Modern Enterprise Business Intelligence and Data Management

Modern Enterprise Business Intelligence and Data Management

A Roadmap for IT Directors, Managers, and Architects

Alan Simon

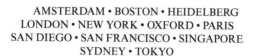

AMSTERDAM • BOSTON • HEIDELBERG
LONDON • NEW YORK • OXFORD • PARIS
SAN DIEGO • SAN FRANCISCO • SINGAPORE
SYDNEY • TOKYO

Morgan Kaufmann is an imprint of Elsevier

Acquiring Editor: Steve Elliot
Editorial Project Manager: Kaitlin Herbert
Project Manager: Mohana Natarajan

Morgan Kaufmann is an imprint of Elsevier
225 Wyman Street, Waltham, MA 02451, USA

Notices
Knowledge and best practice in this field are constantly changing. As new research and
experience broaden our understanding, changes in research methods, professional practices,
or medical treatment may become necessary.

Practitioners and researchers must always rely on their own experience and knowledge in
evaluating and using any information, methods, compounds, or experiments described herein.
In using such information or methods they should be mindful of their own safety and the safety
of others, including parties for whom they have a professional responsibility.

To the fullest extent of the law, neither the Publisher nor the authors, contributors, or editors,
assume any liability for any injury and/or damage to persons or property as a matter of products
liability, negligence or otherwise, or from any use or operation of any methods, products,
instructions, or ideas contained in the material herein.

British Library Cataloguing-in-Publication Data
A catalogue record for this book is available from the British Library.

Library of Congress Cataloging-in-Publication Data
A catalogue record for this book is available from the Library of Congress.

ISBN: 978-0-12-801539-1

For information on all MK publications
visit our website at www.mkp.com

TABLE OF CONTENTS

TERMINOLOGY

One of the primary challenges to the art and science of enterprise data management is that practitioners often disagree about the scope and scale of "enterprise" or what types of data should be considered for management under the umbrella of a given initiative. This brief Preface defines *enterprise data management* from the context that we'll be using throughout this book.

Defining "Enterprise"

Surprisingly, defining an *enterprise* for the purposes of managing data is not necessarily a straightforward matter. In the most general sense, one might think of an enterprise as an entire company; or, in the public sector, an entire governmental agency.

The complicating factor is that some companies and governmental agencies are modest-sized, but others are significantly larger. For modest-sized ones, the "entire company" (or "entire agency") categorization may well be an accurate fit. For example, a company headquartered in a single U.S. city with no remote offices, and with a single product line or brand, may well be thought of in its entirety as an enterprise, even if annual revenues might be approaching $1 billion U.S.

Conversely, consider a company with half the revenues – say, $500 million U.S. – that has been cobbled together through acquisition; which has seven or eight offices across the country; and which has three or four very disjoint lines of business (LOBs) that rarely exchange customer lists and product information and don't share supply chains across the various LOBs. Whereas this company may be a single legal entity for tax and legal purposes, from the standpoint of managing data it may well be an exercise in futility to consider this company as only a single enterprise. Instead, the company may be better thought of as a microcosm of a multinational, multibusiness corporation where it may be more appropriate to focus on a smaller, subcompany unit for an enterprise data management roadmap.

Chapter 2 discusses why determining the scope and scale of a particular enterprise is very important as the starting point for assessing the current state of enterprise data management. A general rule of thumb is to draw the boundaries of an enterprise where you find great deal of data interchange across applications and systems, and where critically important reports and analytics typically draw their data from a collection of databases, file systems, spreadsheets, etc.

Conversely, if you were to look at a given company or governmental agency and find very little sharing of data or integrated reporting across a given collection of data stores and applications, you are better off subdividing the overall organization into multiple enterprises, each of which should be treated individually as you build an enterprise data management roadmap.

Defining "Data"

For the purposes of modern enterprise data management, we need to disregard many of the demarcations made over the years with regards to different classes of data and the usage of those data. Specifically, an enterprise data management initiative must take into consideration:

- *Both structured and unstructured data*: Traditional data management initiatives have focused primarily on structured data such as numeric data; dates; character strings; Boolean fields; enumerated data types; codes; etc. The reason was largely because of the capabilities of first-generation relational database management systems (RDBMSs) and their database ancestors from the 1960s, 1970s, and early 1980s (specifically, hierarchical DBMSs such as IBM's IMS and network DBMSs such as Cullinet's IDMS). Unstructured data such as audio, video, images, compound documents, e-mails, etc. were typically treated separately over the years under various umbrellas such as *knowledge management systems* and *content management systems*. At best, the metadata from unstructured data might be linked to corresponding structured data within a given enterprise data management framework. With the advent of the Big Data era and the convergence of structured and unstructured data for many analytical purposes, we need to disregard the historical demarcation between structured and unstructured data as we build our roadmaps.

- *All levels of data granularity*: Many organizations find that a significant number of their data-related pain points result from the processing that takes place when lowest-level transactional data is summarized, aggregated, and cross-referenced before inclusion in reports or being available to users via business intelligence (BI) tools. In many cases, a lowest-level transactional data element is fundamentally correct but as business rules are applied to that data and the data is aggregated or cross-referenced with other elements to create new "higher-level" data (e.g., monthly sales summaries; customer profitability measures; etc.), errors of various types may be introduced. Therefore, an organization's approach to enterprise data management must take a look at both "raw" and "refined" data.

- *Both transactional and analytical/reporting data*: Many enterprise data management initiatives begin with a declaration along the lines of "we're not going to focus on the transactional data because that's under the control of the various software packages; instead we will focus on the data warehousing environment, where we can control the data." The problem with this demarcation between data from the operational systems and that contained within data warehouses, data marts, operational data stores (ODSs), statistical data sets, etc. is that many of the pain points inherent in the analytical and reporting space are best resolved within the operational systems and the transactional data under their control. Therefore, the enterprise data roadmap must take transactional data from operational systems into consideration, even when many or most of those operational systems might be commercial software packages...or, increasingly, cloud-based operational software not even under the management of an enterprise's IT organization.

- *Both original and duplicated/replicated data*: Most enterprises still find themselves with a high degree of both controlled data replication and uncontrolled data duplication. Data might be fed from a centralized data warehouse into one or more data marts; "spreadmarts" are loaded with data from both operational systems and data marts; etc. A modern enterprise data management roadmap must be cognizant of the duplication/replication footprint throughout a company or governmental agency as specific projects and initiatives are put in place.

Essentially, the enterprise data management roadmap must take "all things data" into consideration, breaking through long-held divisions and demarcations between different types of data.

Defining "Enterprise Data Management"

Given the above definitions of *enterprise* and *data* for purposes of this book, what then do we mean by *enterprise data management*? Simply stated, our primary objective is to bring order and discipline to the manner in which any given organization manages its data.

Further, the specifics of "order and discipline" will vary from any given company or governmental agency to another. Each individual enterprise data management roadmap must be *grounded in the reality of that particular enterprise*. Technology, work processes, organizational structure, organizational culture, upcoming major business initiatives... all of these and more must be carefully considered as plans and roadmaps take shape.

Defining "Business Intelligence"

Many business and IT professionals have a rigid, almost dogmatic view of various forms of data-driven reporting and insights. They draw a distinction between reporting and querying; operational versus strategic business intelligence; business intelligence versus analytics; reports from operational systems versus reports produced by a data warehouse or data mart; and so on.

For purposes of a well-structured enterprise data management roadmap, *all* forms of data access and delivery should be included for consideration, essentially sidestepping dissension over, for example, what constitutes "business intelligence" versus "analytics." Throughout this book we will use "business intelligence" as an umbrella term and as necessary, insert specific demarcations when considering unique patterns and types of information access and delivery to users and analytical applications.

ABOUT THE AUTHOR

Alan Simon is a Senior Lecturer in the Information Systems Department at Arizona State University's WP Carey School of Business. He is also the Managing Principal of Thinking Helmet, Inc., a boutique consultancy specializing in enterprise business intelligence and data management architecture.

Alan has authored or coauthored 29 technology and business books dating back to 1985. He has previously led national or global BI and data warehousing practices at several consultancies, and has provided enterprise data management architecture and roadmap services to more than 40 clients dating back to the early 1990s. From 1987 to 1992 Alan was a software developer and product manager with Digital Equipment Corporation's Database Systems Group, and earlier he was a United States Air Force Computer Systems Officer stationed at Cheyenne Mountain, Colorado.

Alan received his Bachelor's Degree from Arizona State University and his Master's Degree from the University of Arizona, and is a native of Pittsburgh.

CHAPTER 1

The Rebirth of Enterprise Data Management

1.1 IN THE BEGINNING: HOW WE GOT TO WHERE WE ARE TODAY

Those who cannot remember the past, are condemned to repeat it.
- George Santayana (1863–1952)

To best understand the state of enterprise data management (EDM) today, it's important to understand how we arrived at this point during a journey that dates back nearly 50 years to the days when enormous, expensive mainframe computers were the backbone of "data processing" (as Information Technology was commonly referred to long ago) and computing technology was still in its adolescence.

1.1.1 1960s and 1970s

Many data processing textbooks of the 1960s and 1970s proposed a vision much like that depicted in Figure 1.1.

The simplified architecture envisioned by many prognosticators called for a single common "data base"[1] that would provide a single primary store of data for core business applications such as accounting (general ledger, accounts payable, accounts receivable, payroll, etc.), finance, personnel, procurement, and others. One application might write a new record into the data base that would then be used by another application.

In many ways, this "single data base" vision is similar to the capabilities offered today by many enterprise systems vendors in which a consolidated store of data underlies enterprise resource planning (ERP), customer relationship management (CRM), supply chain management (SCM), human capital management (HCM), and other applications that have touch-points with one another. Under this architecture the typical

---

[1] In the early days of computing, "data base" – two words – was more commonly used than the single word "database" that is used almost universally today.

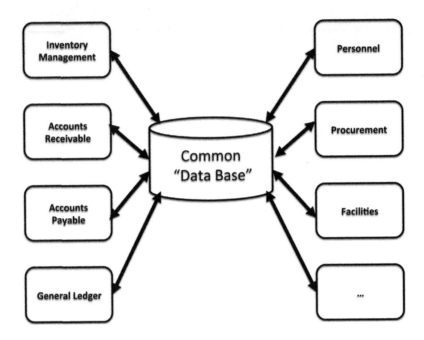

Fig. 1.1. 1960s/1970s vision of a common "data base."

company or governmental agency would face far fewer conflicting data definitions and semantics; conflicting business rules; unnecessary data duplication; and other hindrances than what is found in today's organizational data landscape.

Despite this vision of a highly ordered, quasi-utopian data management architecture, the result for most companies and governmental agencies looked far more like the diagram in Figure 1.2, with each application "owning" its own file systems, tapes, and first-generation database management systems (DBMSs).

Even when an organization's portfolio of applications was housed on a single mainframe, the vision of a shared pool of data among those applications was typically nowhere in the picture. However, the various applications – many of which were custom-written in those days – still needed to share data among themselves. For example, Accounts Receivable and Accounts Payable applications needed to feed data into the General Ledger application. Most organizations found themselves rapidly slipping into the "spider's web quagmire" of numerous one-by-one data exchange interfaces as depicted in Figure 1.3.

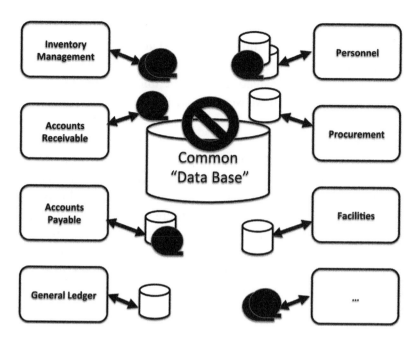

Fig. 1.2. The reality of most 1960s/1970s data environments.

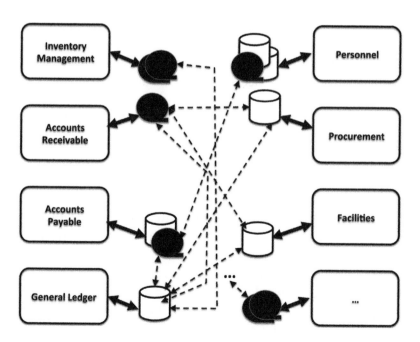

Fig. 1.3. Ungoverned data integration via proliferating one-by-one interfaces.

By the time the 1970s drew to a close and computing was becoming more and more prevalent within business and government, any vision of managing one's data assets at an enterprise level was far from a reality for most organizations. Instead, a world of uncoordinated, often conflicting data silos was what we were left with.

1.1.2 1980s

As the 1980s progressed, the data silo problem actually began to worsen. Minicomputers had been introduced in the 1960s and had grown in popularity during the 1970s, led by vendors such as Digital Equipment Corporation (DEC) and Data General. Increasingly, the fragmentation of both applications and data moved from the realm of the mainframe into minicomputers as organizations began deploying core applications on these newer, smaller-scale platforms. Consequently, the one-by-one file transfers and other types of data exchange depicted in Figure 1.3 were now increasingly occurring across hardware, operating system platforms, and networks, many of which were only beginning to "talk" to one another. As the 1980s proceeded and personal computers (often called "microcomputers" at the time) grew wildly in popularity, the typical enterprise's data architecture grew even more fragmented and chaotic.

Many organizations realized that they now were facing a serious problem with their fragmented data silos, as did many of the leading technology vendors. Throughout the 1980s, two major approaches took shape in an attempt to overcome the fragmentation problem:

- Enterprise data models
- Distributed database management systems (DDBMSs)

1.1.2.1 Enterprise Data Models

Companies and governmental agencies attempted to get their arms around their own data fragmentation problems by embarking on *enterprise data model* initiatives. Using conceptual and logical data modeling techniques that began in the 1970s such as *entity-relationship modeling*, teams of data modelers would attempt to understand and document the enterprise's *existing* data elements and attributes as well as the details of relationships among those elements. The operating premise governing these efforts was that by investing the time and resources to analyze, understand, and document all of the enterprise's data across any number of barriers – application, platform, and organizational, in particular – the "data chaos" would begin to dissipate and new systems could be built leveraging the data structures, relationships, and data-oriented business rules that already existed.

While many enterprise data modeling initiatives did produce a better understanding of an organization's data assets than before a given initiative had begun, these efforts largely withered over time and tended not to yield anywhere near the economies of scale originally envisioned at project inception. The application portfolio of the typical organization in the 1980s was both fast-growing and very volatile, and an enterprise data modeling initiative almost certainly fell behind new and rapidly changing data under the control of any given application or system. The result even before completion, most enterprise data models became "stale" and outdated, and were quietly mothballed.

(As most readers know, data modeling techniques are still widely used today, although primarily as part of the up-front analysis and design phase for a specific software development or package implementation project rather than attempting to document the entire breadth of an enterprise's data assets.)

1.1.2.2 Distributed Database Management Systems (DDBMSs)

Enterprise data modeling efforts on the parts of companies and governmental agencies were primarily an attempt to *understand* an organization's highly fragmented data. The data models themselves did nothing to help facilitate the integration of data across platforms, databases, organizational boundaries, etc.

To address the data fragmentation problem from an integration perspective, most of the leading computer companies and database vendors of the 1980s began work on *DDBMSs*. The specific technical approaches from companies such as IBM (Information Warehouse), Digital Equipment Corporation (RdbStar), Ingres (Ingres Star), and others varied from one to another, but the fundamental premise of most DDBMS efforts was as depicted in Figure 1.4.

The DDBMS story went like this: regardless of how scattered an organization's data might be, a single data model-driven interface could

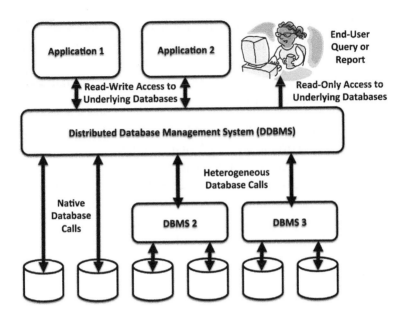

Fig. 1.4. The DDBMS concept.

sit between applications and end-users and the underlying databases, including those from other vendors operating under different DBMSs (#2 and #3 in Figure 1.4). The DDBMS engine would provide *location and platform transparency* to abstract applications and users from the underlying data distribution and heterogeneity, and *both* read-write access as well as read-only access to the enterprise's data through the DDBMS would be possible.

For a number of reasons the DDBMS approach of the late 1980s faltered. Computing technology of the day wasn't robust or powerful enough to handle the required levels of cross-referencing, filtering, and other data management operations across vast networks. Consequently, the state of the art in distributed transaction management to allow relational database COMMIT and ROLLBACK operations across multiple physical databases – and in particular, multiple databases under the control of heterogeneous DBMSs – became the undoing of the DDBMS movement. Other reasons also came into play that are beyond the scope of our discussion here; but the key takeaway is that as the 1980s gave way to the 1990s, organizations were still left with an enterprise data fragmentation problem that was becoming worse by the year.

1.1.3 1990s

Throughout the 1980s and even back into the 1970s, many organizations built *extract files* that pulled select data from an operational system and loaded the data into a separate file system or database to produce reports. The primary reason for creating duplicate data was to avoid adversely impacting the operational systems, which were usually finely tuned to achieve the best possible performance with the technology of the day. With this in mind, two new approaches sprouted in the early 1990s:

- Data warehousing
- Read-only distributed data access

1.1.3.1 Data Warehousing

The more popular and long-lasting of the two by far was the *data warehouse*, which essentially was taking the extract file approach of the 1970s and 1980s and adding a great deal more rigor and discipline to how organizations copied data from source systems into a separate "reporting database."

Whereas most reporting databases pulled data from only one or two source applications to produce a precisely targeted set of reports, the data warehousing concept was originally envisioned by most early proponents to be enterprise wide in scale. Figure 1.5 depicts the *typical enterprise data warehouse* (EDW) attempt of the early 1990s, with the vast majority of any given organization's key applications feeding data into the EDW... which would then be the primary source for reporting and other data access needs for the majority of users and needs across the enterprise.

Even though an EDW appears to be a straightforward proposition, project cost and schedule overruns, as well as outright failures, in the early and mid-1990s were fairly common. EDWs failed for a number of reasons, and not all of those reasons had to do with database technology or underperforming/overpromising first-generation business intelligence (BI) tools. EDW initiatives ran into problems in the 1990s for many of the same reasons they run into problems today: scoping problems, master data management (MDM) discrepancies, data governance conflicts, and the other issues addressed in this book.

While EDWs only made slight headway in addressing the overall problem of EDM, the discipline did establish enough of a beachhead

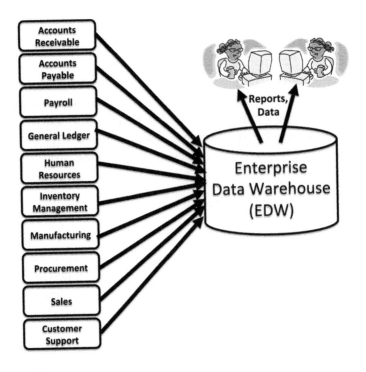

Fig. 1.5. The EDW vision.

and gained enough inertia that we still have enterprise data warehousing as a key weapon in today's and tomorrow's efforts to once and for all make headway in addressing our enterprise data challenges.

1.1.3.2 Read-Only Distributed Data Access

Even as data warehousing and its companion discipline BI gained in popularity throughout the early and mid-1990s, some technologists rebelled against the concept of copying data into a separate database where reports and analytics would then be run. To their way of thinking, storage was still a somewhat precious commodity, and duplicating data was a costly prospect. Further, each extraction, transformation, and loading (ETL) job to copy data from one or more source systems into a data warehouse was ripe for introducing errors and anomalies in the data. (Never mind that the quality of the original-form data housed in many applications was itself highly suspect.)

Taking a fresh look at the failure of DDBMSs of the 1980s and with regards to our earlier discussion, the belief emerged that DDBMSs had failed primarily because they were built to be read-write environments rather than read-only. By removing "write" operations from the DDBMS picture, the thinking went, the synthesized data model sitting on top of multiple underlying databases would therefore be able to help address the data fragmentation problem, at least for reporting and data access.

Many of the DDBMS vendors repurposed their platforms into read-only environments as alternatives to the copying-based approach of data warehousing. DEC, for example, attempted to repurpose its RdbStar DDBMS into a new environment called the *Information Network*. A *Computerworld* article in September, 1992[2] noted that:

> DEC officials also spoke about the remnants of the earlier RdbStar distributed database technology, now referred to as the Information Network. They hope to release a version of the product by early 1993 that will act as a manager of heterogeneous RDBMSs so that users will be able to access and manage data located across a range of databases.

Other vendors such as Information Builders with their Enterprise Data Access (EDA)/SQL product joined in the approach to "virtual data warehousing" as an alternative to what we might term "physical data warehousing," as discussed in the previous section. The virtual data warehousing approach didn't gain much traction as the 1990s progressed, but has remained a niche player over the years. In the mid-2000s, *enterprise information integration* (EII) capabilities were offered by some vendors, and the basic concept has evolved into today's *data virtualization* capabilities offered by a number of vendors.

Essentially, read-only distributed data access and its generational successors attempted to address a large part of the EDM fragmentation problem by overlaying many different underlying databases and their respective DBMSs with a unified, understandable, and well-governed layer that supports the mapping into whatever physical topology quagmire exists underneath.

Even as organizations tried to gain a foothold with their EDM problems, even more challenges resulted (albeit inadvertently) from the Y2K problem. Companies and governmental agencies had a choice

---

[2] "Global buffering beefs up Rdb," *Computerworld*, September 21, 1992, p. 16.

between two different approaches to addressing Y2K as the clock ticked down:

1. Remediate (patch and fix) existing custom and packaged software to correct any two-digit date issues in the code; or
2. Replace outdated legacy software with modern, Y2K-compliant software packages...typically ERP software from vendors such as SAP, Oracle, PeopleSoft, and others.

Given the urgency of the Y2K problem, many organizations who chose option #2 – replacing legacy applications with well-architected ERP software – were so focused on beating the Y2K clock that they didn't have the time, personnel, or financial resources to take advantage of the rare opportunity to address their EDM challenges at the same time. These organizations were also trying to come to grips with the first generation of eCommerce as well as new CRM systems and SCM applications, and with all that was going on in most organizations it isn't surprising that data architecture and governance took a back seat to getting systems installed.

Most organizations had every intention of addressing EDM – as well as integrating their new enterprise systems, and a host of other on-the-books initiatives – after Y2K came and went.

1.1.4 2000s

Between early 2000 and late 2002, the global economy was subjected to:

- The dot-com meltdown;
- The aftermath of the 9/11 terrorist attacks, including deep budget cuts in many companies and governmental agencies as the economy continued to slow;
- The fallout from the accounting and business scandals of the early 2000s (Enron, Tyco, WorldCom, and others) that did further damage to the overall economy and business budgets.

For close to 3 years, many organizations retrenched into "maintenance mode" in which they focused their efforts largely on break-fix support work, with significant cutbacks in enhancing and integrating their new systems...not to mention putting many initiatives that fell under the EDM umbrella on the back burner. Data warehousing-type projects continued to get scaled back to more modest *data marts* that often successfully addressed specific reporting and analysis needs...but also increased the data fragmentation and reporting silo problem. Mantras from the 1990s and the dawn of the BI/data warehousing modern era such as "seeking a single version of the truth" were as distant a dream as ever for most organizations in the early 2000s.

By early 2004, most economies around the world had recovered sufficiently that technology spending increased and organizations once again began to take a critical look at their EDM problems. Some organizations made significant progress over the next couple of years, while others were far less successful. But regardless of the gains any given organization did or didn't achieve in the 2004–2008 timeframe, the Great Recession that began in late 2008 had an even more severe impact on technology investment for most companies than the recession at the beginning of the decade. Even though conventional wisdom holds that the actual recession was over by mid-2009, the severity of the downturn resulted in overall suppressed technology investments for several more years.

And all the while, organizations continued to struggle through many of the same EDM challenges that they've faced for decades.

1.1.5 Today

For most businesses and governmental agencies, the Great Recession is behind us. Technology investment is on the upswing, and has been for several years. The Big Data Era is upon us, with an entirely new portfolio of high-capacity, high-velocity technology available for a new generation of data management. More importantly, we have a quarter century's worth of best practices, success stories, and lessons learned to draw from.

Further, many organizations are finally coming to grips with the realization that failure to get their EDM house in order is a recipe for even greater chaos than they may have experienced in the past. Data volumes are exploding, and even if organizations can apply data warehousing appliances and Big Data technologies and architecture to deal with the data volumes, meaningful progress will be hard to come by without an accompanying well-formulated EDM roadmap.

Chapter 5 contains further discussion about today's – and tomorrow's – data management architecture; we will look at the concept of the Big Data-driven "data lake" and various architectural options for how "data lakes" either coexist or supplant traditional data warehousing. Stay tuned.

1.2 A MANIFESTO FOR MODERN ENTERPRISE DATA MANAGEMENT: WHAT ARE WE TRYING TO ACCOMPLISH?

A long-standing challenge to the typical organization embarking on an EDM initiative is the lack of consensus on the answer to one very straightforward question:

What are we trying to accomplish?

Below is a concise "manifesto" for EDM that all executives, strategists, and lead technologists should have in mind when beginning to formulate an EDM roadmap. By filtering down your overarching objectives to a very concise, manageable number – in this case, four – it's easier to keep an initiative on track despite the fact that the effort *will* quickly become steeped in technical challenges, organizational politics, and other complications.

The four objectives of any EDM initiative should be:

1. Eliminating chaos and bringing order to data, reporting, and analytics
2. Building a foundation that best supports other emerging technologies and new or enhanced applications
3. Converting slogans about the "goodness" of data from trite sayings to reality
4. Ensuring that whatever approach your roadmap does specify is appropriately aligned with your organization's structure and culture

1.2.1 Bringing Order to an Organization's Data, Reporting, and Analytics

The history presented in this chapter is indicative of the current state of EDM for many companies and governmental agencies, and one word can be used to sum up their respective states: *chaos*. For all of the reasons discussed in this chapter, most large-scale enterprises that have been in existence for at least a quarter century currently deal with fragmentation of data across many different databases, file systems, and mission-critical spreadsheets. They are hampered by conflicting data definitions and business rules. Big Data is seen as important for the future, but there is a lack of consensus about how Big Data fits alongside traditional data warehousing and BI. A thick layer of tension overlays many discussions about data, reports, analytics, Key Performance Indicators (KPIs), etc.

Even smaller or newer enterprises still often find themselves with many of the same challenges and tensions that larger and longer-lived organizations do. In general, unless an organization placed a very high degree of importance on EDM from the first days of its existence – and it's rare to find an organization that did – a lack of order and discipline will hallmark its overall data environment.

The ultimate target of an EDM effort should *never* be a utopian state akin to that depicted in Figure 1.1. Even if a single data store does turn out to be the center-point of an organization's enterprise systems portfolio, they almost certainly will still have data marts, data warehouses, ancillary applications, report-producing spreadsheets, etc. in the overall landscape. The goal should be that regardless of the topology, adequate order and sensibility hallmark the environment rather than chaos and dissension.

1.2.2 Supporting Emerging Technologies and New or Enhanced Applications

From in-memory databases to columnar databases to other advanced data management capabilities, the pace of advances in the tools and technologies at our disposal seems to be increasing. On the application side, the major enterprise systems vendors regularly add functional modules and increase the level of integration and interoperability among their existing products.

Organizations of all types and sizes can benefit from these advances, but very often they find their efforts compromised by the haphazard, chaotic state of their data assets: inconsistent master data; conflicting business rules; uncontrolled data proliferation; etc.

Conversely, organizations with a solidly architected EDM landscape often find that experimenting with new technologies and integrating new application functionality is a far less strenuous, less problematic effort than if chaos and confusion hallmarked their data assets.

1.2.3 Turning "Data is our Lifeblood" and "The Data-Driven Organization" into More than Just Slogans

One doesn't have to look very far to find slogans such as "data is our company's lifeblood" or "we strive to become a data-driven organization" as part of a given company's or governmental agency's vision statements. Too often, although, these slogans ring hollow when one looks at the underlying state of that organization's data and how information is managed and governed.

The subject of this book – a roadmap to well-architected EDM – is the first step in turning these slogans from jargon to reality.

1.2.4 Aligning Our Approach and Architecture with Our Organizational Structure and Culture

Beyond the size and scope of any given company or governmental agency (see *Defining "Enterprise"* earlier in this chapter), an organization's EDM roadmap *must* be aligned with their structure and culture to have a chance of being successfully executed.

For example, an EDM roadmap that calls for highly centralized data stores and autocratic, almost dictatorial governance policies will almost certainly turn into an exercise in futility if applied to a company that is very decentralized and empowerment-oriented at lower levels of the organization. Branch managers, division heads, and other Directors or Vice Presidents (or even lower levels within the organization) are likely to bristle and even rebel at the first hints of "being told what to do with *their* data."

As discussed in subsequent chapters, a great deal of thought and effort needs to occur at all points along the preparation of an EDM roadmap to help align the recommended future state, milestones, declarations of success, and other factors with the structure and culture of that particular enterprise.

1.3 CHAPTER SUMMARY

Make no mistake about it: *real* EDM is a very challenging proposition. The past 50 years of technology and business history has created significant inertia that has served to thwart all but a handful of EDM initiatives, leaving the typical organization with a current state of its data management that may be categorized as "troubled," "chaotic," "dysfunctional," or some other negative connotation.

All the while, the precious commodities of time, money, and effort are increasingly diverted to unnecessary activities such as repeatedly trying to understand why two or three reports that should show the same results actually don't. Or late-night, long-hour heroics to produce *correct* mission-critical or regulatory reports have become a regular occurrence rather than the exception.

The first step toward successful EDM is to understand how we've arrived at where we are today. Armed with this knowledge, we can then begin to assess *exactly* where we are in any given organization, and move forward from that point.

CHAPTER 2

Assessing Your Organization's Current State of Enterprise Data Management

2.1 INTRODUCTION

Every journey begins by understanding where you are.

The above phrase, or any one of dozens of variations, describes perfectly the starting point in building a grounded-in-reality enterprise data management (EDM) roadmap: specifically, conducting a comprehensive assessment of that enterprise's current EDM state.

Too often, though, current state assessments get bogged down in excruciating detail; or they get sidetracked for one reason or another; or in general, get a roadmap effort of any type off to a less-than-desirable start.

This chapter will describe a two-step process through which you can *quickly* assess the health – or lack thereof – of a handful of key evaluation factors related to the current state of EDM.

2.2 A RAPID, CONSENSUS-DRIVEN STARTING POINT TO CURRENT STATE ASSESSMENT

A successful current state assessment for EDM:

- Is accomplished quickly
- Gathers input from a large number of participants from many different job levels in different organizations and functions throughout the enterprise
- Is conducted in a manner in which objective data collection and results can transcend organizational politics, "the loudest voices," etc.

The recommended assessment approach is comprised of two steps:

1. Deciding what the scope and scale of the enterprise under consideration should be; and
2. Using a scorecard-based methodology to collect, synthesize, and report assessment results.

2.2.1 Step 1: Determining the Scope and Scale of the Enterprise

Simply stated, any one enterprise may vary greatly from another with regards to the scope and scale of its business operations. While this may seem to be a statement of the obvious, when it comes to the starting point for an EDM current state assessment – or for the EDM roadmap effort as a whole – this step cannot be overlooked.

Consider the following two companies:

- **Company #1** is in the health club industry, with its headquarters based in Denver, Colorado. The company operates health clubs in major cities across the United States under a single brand. Most of the health clubs offer the same equipment and services (e.g., Yoga and aerobic classes; personal training; nutritional consulting; etc.), although some of the facilities are also used for test marketing new equipment and services. The company began to expand internationally 2 years earlier, but all international locations operate under the same brand as in the United States with mostly similar equipment and services. The company recently passed $1 billion (U.S.) in annual revenue, which continues to grow at 15–20%/year.

  The company runs all of its IT systems out of the Denver headquarters office (which is the only company location other than the health clubs themselves), and runs its operations from a single integrated suite of ERP, CRM, and other enterprise systems.

- **Company #2** is a global retailer that has grown by acquisition over the past decade, as well as organically. Currently the company has four different brands aimed at different market segments. Each brand operates in a largely autonomous manner, with a Brand President as the primary decision-maker. Two of the company's brands have stores in the United States, EMEA (Europe/Middle East/Africa), and APAC (Asia/Pacific) regions; a third brand is United States and EMEA only (no APAC); and the fourth brand is EMEA and APAC only, at least for now.

  The company's corporate headquarters are in the Los Angeles metro area, but Brand 2 (an acquisition) maintains its primary operations in Chicago while Brand 4 (another acquisition) – which doesn't currently have U.S. stores – has its EMEA operations run from Paris and separately, APAC operations run from Tokyo.

Most of the brands also operate regional headquarters, although the regional alignment differs widely from one brand to another.

Across the brands and locations one will find six different ERP systems from multiple vendors; brand-specific CRM systems that currently do not exchange customer data among themselves; and brand-specific supply chain management (SCM) systems. The company's annual revenues are around $9 billion (U.S.).

In the case of Company #1, it's easy to see how the "enterprise" can *and should* apply to the entire company. The product and service line-up, operational processes, organizational structure and culture...all are aligned very well to address EDM in a company-wide manner.

Company #2, however, is structured – at least currently – more as a federation of loosely related businesses than as a cohesive enterprise. Attempting to develop enterprise-wide uniform master data management (MDM), *true* enterprise-scale data warehousing, and many of the other aspects of EDM (see Chapter 4) in an all-inclusive manner across this particular company would be extremely difficult...and possibly even irrelevant.

Consequently, an EDM effort for Company #2 that begins with a current state assessment would likely be better aligned with its organizational structure and culture by addressing each brand individually; or perhaps EMEA operations across multiple brands; or some other "slice" of the company, rather than Company #2 as a whole.

If, however, Company #2 intends to dramatically increase conformity and cohesion across its brands and geographies, then there may well be merit in tackling a larger scope for an EDM effort than a single brand. The point is that you want an EDM effort set up for success as much as possible, and the starting point to doing so is to select the appropriate scope and scale for the enterprise.

2.2.2 Step 2: Complete a 4-by-4 Assessment Scorecard

Many businesses use the *balanced scorecard* technique to collect and present a (by definition) balanced combination of financial and non-financial indicators to executives and decision-makers. The intention of the balanced scorecard is to allow users to rapidly assess the overall performance of an organization along four different planes against formalized goals:

- Financial
- Customer (i.e., customer expectations and loyalty)
- Internal Business Processes (i.e., efficiencies and quality)
- Learning and Growth (i.e., recruiting and training)

Most representations of the balanced scorecard have a "windmill" appearance with the four different categories as well as the depiction of how the categories relate to one another and how all are aligned with the organization's overall vision and strategy.

The balanced scorecard paradigm is very well-suited to adaptation to an *EDM scorecard* in which four data-related categories – operational reporting and querying; strategic insights; data architecture; and work processes along with human and organizational factors – are scored and easily viewed (Figure 2.1).

As shown in Figure 2.2, each of the four EDM categories contains four different index values, and for the sake of consistency and ease of interpretation, all four values are the same for each of the four categories.

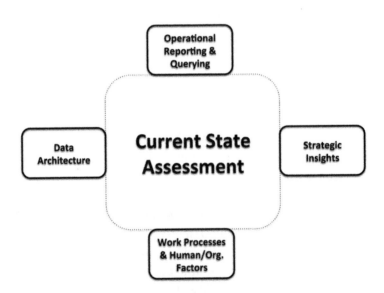

Fig. 2.1. The balanced scorecard-like assessment template.

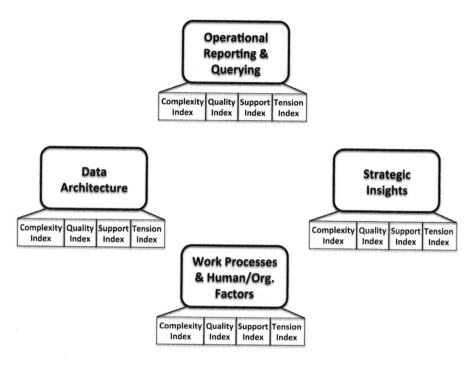

Fig. 2.2. Four-index scoring for each category.

The index values are:

- Complexity
- Quality
- Support
- Tension

Each is described in the sections that follow.

Based on the scores that are collected and averaged, "hot spots" – areas that are particularly problematic – can be identified (Figure 2.3). The methodology for scoring, analyzing, and identifying "hot spots" is discussed later in this chapter.

2.2.2.1 Complexity Index

In general, how *unnecessarily* complex is a given evaluation factor? Complexity is all but a given in modern business technology environments, with numerous components interacting with one another. Some enterprises have done a very good job of streamlining interactions, or

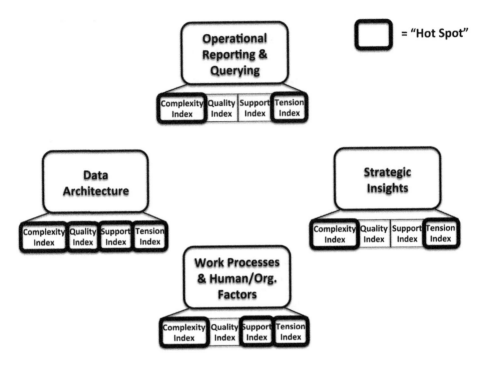

Fig. 2.3. Using scorecard "hot spots" to identify EDM areas of concern.

documenting interfaces and business rules. Other enterprises are hall-marked by poorly documented, archaic manual processes for their data management, internal reporting, business intelligence (BI), etc., all of which have persisted for years.

The sections later in this chapter for each of the evaluation factors provide specific examples of how to evaluate and score complexity.

2.2.2.2 Quality Index

Are the production operational reports coming out of the transactional systems trusted? Are dashboards produced from an organization's data warehouses and data marts rarely used because their accuracy is suspect? Do workers throughout an organization "know that our data is pretty bad?" Is much of the ungoverned, spreadsheet-driven data extraction, and reporting done by individual workers themselves hallmarked by inconsistent business rules, nonstandard data hierarchies, or even outright errors?

As with complexity, the sections later in the chapter guide you in scoring quality for each of the evaluation factors.

2.2.2.3 Support Index

How much of a support burden are operational reports, strategic BI, data warehouse, or data mart ETL jobs, etc.? How quickly and efficiently can requests for new reports and analytics be met? Are there significant "wasted cycles" while waiting for approvals, QA, etc.?

Timely, skilled support should be an inherent characteristic of an organization's EDM capabilities, and the objective during the current state assessment is to see how various categories of support are viewed today.

2.2.2.4 Tension Index

Most readers have experienced heated discussions over which of two (or three or more) reports is correct, when all three should be showing identical results. Or they have experienced the exasperation of needing to quickly implement a critical new report, only to be told by the data warehousing team that there is no way the required data can be brought into the warehouse for at least two more months, no matter how high priority that requirement might be.

Then there's the enterprise data warehousing team who has been building out very solidly architected data structures as part of an expansion of enterprise data warehouse (EDW) functionality, only to learn that several business organizations have quietly built their own data marts and intend to use those siloed, "one-off" solutions rather than the EDW.

EDM is enough of a challenging proposition (as described in Chapter 1) but technical and process-related challenges are often compounded by tremendous interorganizational and interpersonal tensions. Part of the current state assessment effort described in this chapter is to bring these tensions to light so that they may be adequately addressed as part of the roadmap to the target future state.

2.3 CATEGORY 1: OPERATIONAL REPORTING AND QUERYING

Assessments, strategies, and roadmaps are often adversely impacted by matters of semantics. What's the difference – if any – between operational reporting and production reporting? Are operational queries conceptually the same as an ad hoc operational query? Should we include recommendations for operational reports directly from our transactional systems as well as those from an operational data store

(ODS)? If a data warehouse or data mart supports real-time "tell me what is happening right now" forms of analytics, should we include those as well?

For purposes of an EDM roadmap, *any and all* uses of data as part of day-to-day business operations – both routine and exception-driven – should be considered as part of this first scoring category. Remember that at this stage of a roadmap effort, you are focused on quickly consolidating and scoring a consensus opinion to highlight what is currently working well and what isn't. The "why and how" specifics behind those scores certainly will need to be delved into, but doing so can occur in later phases of the roadmap effort, as discussed in Chapter 5.

Further, as depicted in Figure 2.4, respondents should focus their attentions on the operational reports and queries themselves and their usage as they record their scores, putting the other evaluation factors (strategic insights, data architecture, and related work processes/human factors) aside. Each of those categories will be similarly scored, as described in the following sections. But by precisely focusing respondents'

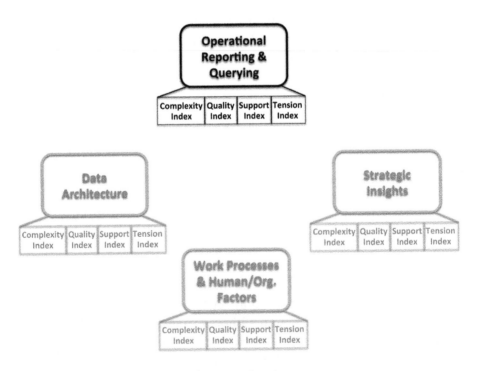

Fig. 2.4. Scoring an organization's operational reporting and querying.

attentions on the operational reports and queries (and then afterwards on the other factors, one by one), "cleaner and clearer" results are likely to be the outcome of the current state assessment.

Table 2.1 describes the three possible scores each of the four categories can receive from each respondent, along with examples for why a given score would be given.

Table 2.1. Scoring the Four Evaluation Factors for Operational Reports and Queries	
Operational Reporting	
Complexity Index	
5 (best)	Most or all operational reports and inquiries don't require multiple manual, time-consuming steps to prepare and deliver; many or most are produced automatically on a scheduled basis, and all are available on demand "at the push of a button."
3	Some operational reports are fully automated but many others require time-consuming manual processes for data extraction from multiple sources and reconciliation of the consolidated data; ad hoc inquiries are particularly challenging, requiring multiple manual steps, and often multiple people to be involved.
1 (worst)	The majority of operational reporting and inquiries are problematic and time-consuming, largely due to a complex topology hallmarked by manual extraction and consolidation, spreadsheet-based reconciliation, etc.
Quality Index	
5 (best)	Operational reports and inquiries are rarely challenged on accuracy.
3	Most key operational reports – especially regulatory ones – don't have quality issues, but others (especially those involving many manual steps) are often suspect and require double-checking before usage or delivery.
1 (worst)	Operational reporting and inquiries are "a mess" – results almost always need to be double-checked and corrected. Reports are often recalled and updated; sanctions letters from governmental or industry-regulating bodies have occurred because of erroneous reports.
Support Index	
5 (best)	Operational reporting is typically a fully automated, "lights out" process with little or no just-in-time support needed from the Help Desk, development teams, etc. A high degree of self-service operational querying occurs throughout the enterprise by end users at all levels of the organization, with little or no assistance required from IT.
3	Most operational reporting is "lights out" and fully automated, but some requires regular and extensive support from IT to meet deadlines, validate results, etc.
1 (worst)	Operational reports are often late because extensive support is needed to produce and deliver them; operational reporting is widely considered a "high-maintenance function" throughout the entire enterprise.
Tension Index	
5 (best)	Because of high quality, manageable complexity, and minimal support, operational reporting and querying is a "low-tension" function within the enterprise. Occasional Help Desk tickets, requests to double-check results, etc. rarely result in tensions flaring.
3	On occasion, tempers do flare over issues with operational reporting, requests for self-service support, etc.
1 (worst)	In general, operational reporting is not only problematic for reasons of quality, complexity, etc., but it's also a regular, high-tension "hot spot" across the enterprise; interorganizational and interpersonal issues further impede the production and usage of operational data.

2.4 CATEGORY 2: STRATEGIC INSIGHTS

Even more so than with operational reporting and querying, the second category of *strategic insights* is fraught with conflicting opinions over terminology. What are the similarities and differences between *business intelligence* and *analytics*? Are *analytics* and *advanced analytics* really the same, or are there subtle differences between the two? What about *business intelligence* versus *business performance management*?

For purposes of a current state assessment, semantic differences between these different *but related* disciplines should be set aside. *All of the above* should be included by respondents when contemplating, evaluating, and then scoring this second category. Essentially, each respondent should include any and all capabilities that he or she is aware of to answer questions, produce reports, or provide critical insights that (Simon, 1997, 2013–2014):

- Tell what happened, and why;
- Tell what is happening right now, and why;
- Tell what is likely to happen, and why;
- Tell what might have happened if we had done something different, and why; and
- Tell something interesting and important without me asking a specific question.

As with the first category of operational reporting and querying, each respondent should focus solely on the enterprise's strategic insights themselves when considering and scoring this category (Figure 2.5).

Table 2.2 describes the three possible scores each of the four categories for strategic insights can receive from each respondent, along with examples for why a given score would be given.

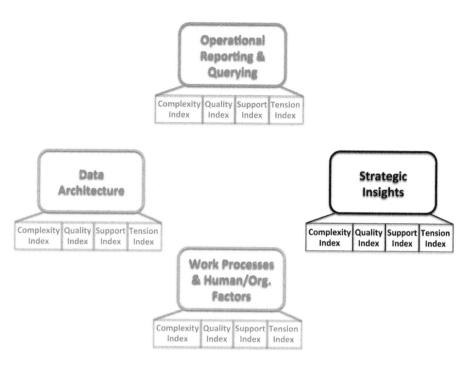

Fig. 2.5. Scoring an organization's strategic insights.

Table 2.2. Scoring the Four Evaluation Factors for Strategic Insights

Strategic Insights

Complexity Index

5 (best)	Even if multiple data marts, data warehouses, and analytic data stores exist throughout the enterprise, or if multiple BI and analytic tools are present, users of BI and analytics are largely abstracted away from the underlying complexity; "insights at your fingertips" is an accurate description of the enterprise's overall strategic BI and analytical capabilities.
3	While some "insights at your fingertips" capabilities exist, many others require significant manual data extraction and manipulation before reports and analytics can be prepared and used.
1 (worst)	BI is "a mess" and Big Data-driven predictive analytics are nowhere on the horizon; the data warehouses and marts, BI tools, etc. make up a patchwork of nonintegrated capabilities; strategic planning is still largely done via spreadsheets and ungoverned manual data extraction, synthesis, etc.

Quality Index

5 (best)	Results on BI reports are largely trusted to be accurate; recommendations from predictive analytics capabilities can be evaluated on their own merits without worrying about the quality of the data that went into the models; etc.
3	Some BI reports are trusted, but factors such as the complexity and inconsistency of undocumented business rules; lack of handling history in slowly changing dimensions (SCDs) for as-was reporting; and inconsistent data cross-referencing cause a substantial portion of the BI to be untrusted.
1 (worst)	"Nobody trusts or even uses the BI reports...we do our own forecasts and planning from spreadsheets. If all of our BI reports were to disappear tomorrow, nobody would care."

(Continued)

Table 2.2. Scoring the Four Evaluation Factors for Strategic Insights *(cont.)*

Support Index	
5 (best)	Even if the enterprise's strategic insights include hundreds of BI-style reports, Big Data-driven predictive analytics, guided analysis, etc., users rarely require "hand-holding" from the Help Desk or other support organizations. Communities, power users, and other structures have largely enabled self-service BI throughout most organizations, and for the most part the data needed by people is available with little or no just-in-time support (e.g., a new data feed) required.
3	While some of the BI and various data mining capabilities are a low-effort proposition, many other capabilities do require significant support. The organization's backlog of support tickets related to BI, predictive analytics, etc. slowly grows week after week, causing many users give up on "official BI" and perform their own strategic insights from spreadsheets and data they extract themselves.
1 (worst)	From the BI tools to the data mining models to the underlying data, almost everything in the realm of "strategic insights" is a high-maintenance proposition, with extensive support needed almost continually.
Tension Index	
5 (best)	The idea of "a single version of the truth" is close to a reality across the enterprise; but even when different results (that should be the same) appear on reports, an orderly process is in place to reconcile the differences and potentially adjust one or both reports to be "apples to apples" – or at least document differing business rules.
3	A constant low-grade tension exists when it comes to BI; new efforts in Big Data-driven insights have seen spotty results, and many in the enterprise grumble that "Big Data is just more hype." In general, value produced by BI, predictive analytics, and other strategic insights is hindered by occasionally flaring tempers.
1 (worst)	Nearly everything related to BI, data mining, etc. is hallmarked by grumbling, arguments, tense e-mails, etc.

2.5 CATEGORY 3: DATA ARCHITECTURE

When scoring the enterprise's data architecture for the third category, *all* stores of data need to be considered…not just data warehouses, data marts, ODSs, Big Data repositories, etc., but also the underlying databases for ERP, CRM, SCM, human capital management (HCM), vertical industry applications, and so on. The objective of scoring this category is to gain an *end-to-end* understanding of the current state of the data architecture, with a particular emphasis on where "weak links" might be occurring even if the overall data architecture is relatively solid.

Again, as depicted in Figure 2.6, respondents should focus their attention on the data architecture and the related examples in Table 2.3 as they produce their scores.

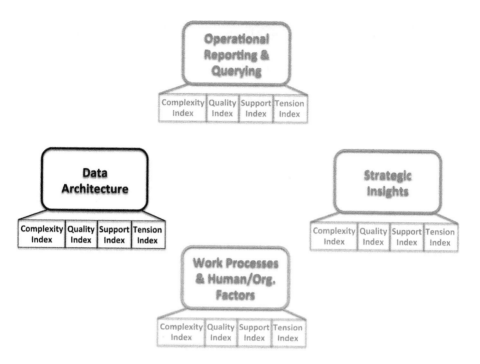

Fig. 2.6. Scoring an organization's data architecture.

Table 2.3. Scoring the Four Evaluation Factors for Data Architecture

Data Architecture

Complexity Index

5 (best)	Even if multiple data marts, data warehouses, and analytic data stores exist throughout the enterprise, an orderly, well-documented, and well-maintained flow of data exists among the many interacting components…including operational systems. Throughout the enterprise, business and IT people alike have a good understanding of what functions are accomplished against which data stores. Duplications of data (via ETL, replication, data ingestion into Big Data engines, etc.) are all orderly and well governed.
3	Some of the data architecture is orderly and well documented, but systems such as organization-specific data marts that acquire their own data; spreadmarts that have proliferated over the years; etc. have eroded the understandability of the overall data landscape. "uncontrolled duplication of data" is a more accurate description than "controlled replication and architected interchanges."
1 (worst)	"Absolutely a mess…enough said." unused data warehouses and governed data marts; so much proliferation of spreadmarts and data extracts that "nobody knows where the data lives."

(Continued)

Table 2.3. Scoring the Four Evaluation Factors for Data Architecture *(cont.)*	
Quality Index	
5 (best)	For the most part, data is trusted across the enterprise in operational systems as well as analytical/reporting data stores (e.g., data warehouses, data marts). Even when spreadmarts are used, they are known to be correct in their data and adherence to business rules.
3	Operational systems have some erroneous data, but "we know where the problems are" and problematic data is cleansed before being used by an application or presented to a user in a report or query. For the most part, data warehouses and data marts have "good enough" data but because they aren't systems of record, the tolerance for problems is higher than might otherwise be advisable.
1 (worst)	"We don't even know how bad our data is" – from outright errors to timing issues to erroneous cross-referencing of data, data is largely untrusted across the entire landscape.
Support Index	
5 (best)	Data interchanges (e.g., ETL jobs) rarely have problems that require human intervention. Performance in operational systems, data warehouses, etc. is almost always within agreed-to specifications, requiring very little trouble-shooting.
3	ETL jobs often require "baby-sitting" to ensure compliance with required data availability deadlines; response time in BI reports and inquiries has been traced to problematic data structures, which in turn requires some level of support for workarounds and patches.
1 (worst)	From the operational systems to the data warehouses, the entire data landscape can only be termed "high maintenance" with an ever-growing backlog of trouble tickets, frequent late hours by developers and support staff to develop workarounds, etc.
Tension Index	
5 (best)	Few if any conflicts arise over who "owns" certain data; where certain data should be housed and stewarded; etc.
3	Turf wars exist regarding usage of data marts and other data stores, and data lineage among the various systems is increasingly murky.
1 (worst)	Simply mentioning "data" almost always causes tempers to flare; attempts to address data issues rarely get anywhere because of interorganizational and interpersonal issues that also impede the effectiveness and efficiency of the business as a whole.

2.6 CATEGORY 4: WORK PROCESSES AND HUMAN/ORGANIZATIONAL FACTORS

The fourth and final evaluation category is for the work processes, organizational and team structures, skills, and other human/organizational factors that surround operational reporting, strategic insights, and data management. Figure 2.7 again emphasizes that when scoring this category respondents should set aside thoughts of reports, analytics, data stores, etc. and instead focus on the evaluation examples described in Table 2.4.

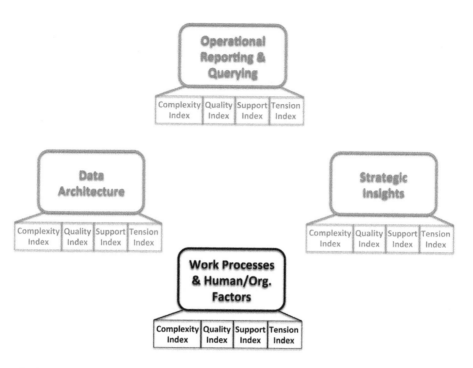

Fig. 2.7. Scoring an organization's work processes, human/organizational factors.

Table 2.4. Scoring the Four Evaluation Factors for Work Processes and Human Factors

Work Processes and Human Factors

Complexity Index

5 (best)	Roles and responsibilities for reporting, data management, support, etc. are widely accepted and well documented through a RACI (responsible/accountable/consulted/informed) matrix or similar formal role-to-responsibility mechanism. Even when many individuals from a number of organizations are involved in a particular data-related effort, the flow of control and information are orderly and efficient.
3	Many roles and responsibilities are agreed to and documented, but others (including critical ones) are less understood and increasingly problematic. "Too many cooks in the kitchen" is an appropriate description of some processes that have become overly complex.
1 (worst)	Most data-related work processes (e.g., assisting a user with a self-service query; troubleshooting a report response time issue; etc.) take too long to accomplish because of unnecessary complexity.

Quality Index

5 (best)	Across the enterprise there is a high degree of trust that data-related activities will conclude with the highest degree of quality. For example, a "one-off" request for a data feed will result in *correct* data being loaded into the target data store and being presented correctly on new reports.

(Continued)

Table 2.4. Scoring the Four Evaluation Factors for Work Processes and Human Factors *(cont.)*	
3	Some development and support processes related to data are trusted, while others often have to be repeated to correct problems. An example of the latter: a business user calling the Help Desk for assistance with self-service BI often receives *incorrect* information for how to build a new report template, set up filters and prompts, etc.
1 (worst)	Most development, support, data interpretation, etc. is problematic and untrusted.
Support Index	
5 (best)	Help Desk support, assistance from power users, and other work processes related to data, reporting, and analytics rarely require supplemental assistance or escalation because assistance can't be provided. From ETL to self-service BI, work flows easily within the enterprise.
3	More often than desired, activities related to data, reporting, and analytics require involvement by additional persons or organizations beyond the "official" role-responsibility alignment. Escalations to gain the additional assistance also occur frequently to address timeliness of responses.
1 (worst)	The enterprise is hallmarked by "dead end" processes related to data, reporting, and analytics, resulting in an ever-growing backlog of critical work activities on the business and IT sides. Employees involved in all aspects of data are typically under-skilled. Often, people don't know exactly who to contact for support with a specific request or problem.
Tension Index	
5 (best)	Well-architected workflows for data-related activities mean that for the most part, the enterprise experiences very few cross-organization or interpersonal tensions for both scheduled and exception-driven activities.
3	Usually requests for assistance as well as scheduled workflows are tension-free, but not always.
1 (worst)	An organization hallmarked by ill-designed workflows and unskilled staff members for data-related activities also means that on a daily basis, interpersonal and cross-organization tensions are readily apparent and further serve to impede the organization's data management and usage capabilities.

2.7 BUILDING AND GRADING THE 4-BY-4 SCORECARD

Blank scorecards should be distributed as widely as possible throughout the enterprise. The objective is to reach a critical mass of individuals in as many organizations as possible on both the business and IT sides of the enterprise. Essentially, anyone in the enterprise – at any employment level, from a CxO to a database administrator (DBA) – should be polled for that individual's perspectives.

Organizations may wish to use an online survey tool for both ease and accuracy of data collection as well as supporting anonymity of responders. In addition to allowing responders to enter their 5-3-1 scores for each of the evaluation criteria, an *optional* free text box should accompany each entry to allow a responder to elaborate on his or her reasoning for any given score. However, since the primary purpose of this exercise is to make an initial determination of the "data hot spots" that exist within the enterprise, commentary verbiage should be optional to allow someone to complete the survey in approximately 5 minutes simply by selecting the appropriate score for each factor and not taking the time to type specific examples.

Similarly, an optional Comments Box at the bottom of the survey may be included for a respondent to offer overall commentary.

The grading of the scorecards, once submissions are closed, is a very straightforward proposition. Specifically:

1. Average scores for each of the 16 values will be calculated
2. Any given score that is lower than a 2.5 average will be noted as a potential "data hot spot" meaning that particular attention needs to be paid to these factors as roadmap activity proceeds (see Figure 2.8).

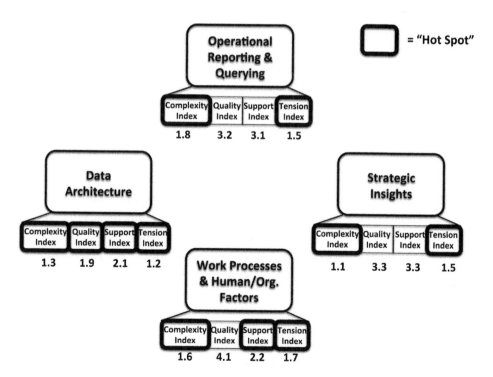

Fig. 2.8. Using average scores to identify "hot spots."

2.8 INTERPRETING THE MEANING OF THE RESULTS

You can very quickly use the consolidated results to formulate several hypotheses:

1. If more than half of the 16 individual scores (4 each for the 4 evaluation factors) show as "hot spots" with an average score less than 2.5, the current EDM environment faces serious problems: top to bottom, and end to end (see Figure 2.8 as an example). That conclusion may very well be the conventional wisdom within the enterprise already, but as a result of the survey results you now have quantifiable "evidence" to that effect. Essentially, the very problematic state of data storage, usage, and governance throughout the enterprise is being brought to light to (hopefully) be addressed, not swept under the proverbial rug.

2. If most of the average scores are relatively high – averages close to or exceeding 4.0 – but three or four individual factors have very *low* scores (under 2.0 average), the roadmap effort can heavily focus on those particular factors as key areas that absolutely must be addressed...and perhaps even need immediate remediation.

3. Even if most or all scores are in the "good" range, those results do *not* mean that the status quo should be maintained, and that a roadmap effort would be a waste of time, resources, and money. As discussed in Chapter 3, key business initiatives across the enterprise may well mean that there is no way the status quo of EDM can or should be maintained. Or, stated another way: key business initiatives in enterprise systems rationalization or lean manufacturing *cannot* succeed on top of the current state of enterprise data, despite the lack of a "burning platform" for change.

4. Finally, incorporation and mainstreaming of Big Data into business workflow and the technology landscape almost certainly means that at the very least, any given organization's enterprise data architecture needs some amount of work to avoid turning Big Data initiatives, predictive analytics, etc. into a poorly architected bolt-on to the current state.

2.9 CHAPTER SUMMARY

A solid roadmap initiative for EDM begins with a dispassionate, introspective, and thorough assessment of that enterprise's current state. By following the approach described in this chapter, strategists can accomplish a current state assessment quickly; objectively; in a straight-forward manner; and driven by input from the largest possible constituency across the organization.

One key item to keep in mind is that the current state assessment is, by definition, a comprehensive look at the state of an organization's EDM *today*. Many organizations have any number of data-related initiatives underway or planned at any given point, which means that even before embarking on an EDM roadmap effort you must also take into consideration what changes – both business process-related and technology – that will impact what you have just finished assessing. Chapter 3 discusses how to inventory key business and technology initiatives that will, along with the results from your current state assessment, factor into your EDM roadmap.

REFERENCES

Simon, A., 1997. Better Tools, Better Decisions, Byte, January.

Simon, A., 2013–2014. Class Lecture Materials, CIS 394: Business Intelligence. Arizona State University, Tempe, Arizona.

Identifying and Cataloguing
Key Business Imperatives

3.1 INTRODUCTION

The work accomplished by the tasks described in Chapter 2 will give organizations a very clear, objective picture of the state of their current enterprise data management (EDM)...with the emphasis on the word "current."

But even as an EDM roadmap effort gets underway, an organization almost always has at least one or two significant business initiatives in progress or are about to start that need to be considered along the timeline of the roadmap leadings toward the future EDM state.

Some business-focused initiatives may have activities that directly or indirectly address enterprise data "hot spots." For example, an *enterprise systems rationalization and consolidation* effort (described later in the chapter) may contain a large body of work to unify key master data subject areas, which in turn will likely dramatically improve the quality and support aspects of operational reporting as well as strategic insights (e.g., business intelligence, predictive analytics, etc.).

Other initiatives may not be explicitly address one or more problem areas, but unless certain "hot spots" are addressed either by separate efforts or by adding a body of work to an in-progress initiative, significant (and previously unforeseen) data-related challenges are inevitable.

Both types of situations described above need to be considered as an EDM roadmap effort proceeds. Essentially, today's current state of EDM may not be the same 6 months from now, or a year from now, as a result of one or more initiatives. Thus, the scoring of the current state (Chapter 2) needs to be tempered by the trajectory of operational reporting, strategic insights, data architecture, and work processes/human factors as determined by what's already underway across the enterprise.

While not an exhaustive list, this chapter does provide a broad sampling of the most common types of business initiatives found today that need to be considered as part of an EDM roadmap effort.

3.2 CROSS-BRAND, CROSS-GEOGRAPHY STRATEGIC SOURCING

Consider the fictional "Company #2" presented at the beginning of Chapter 2: a multibrand, global retailer that has been built in part by acquisition and which is structurally and culturally very empowerment-oriented, with brands running their own supply chain systems and other enterprise software. Further, in the current state, very little exchange of data across the brands occurs, other than consolidation of financial and other data up to the corporate level as required for regulatory reporting.

Given the model presented in Chapter 2 – that attempting to address EDM holistically across all of the individual brands and geographies would likely be an exercise in futility – a more "grounded in reality" approach to an EDM roadmap might be to complete one for each individual brand. However, suppose that corporate-level executive management, with the Board of Directors' backing, has embarked on a multiyear initiative to implement *cross-brand, cross-geography strategic sourcing* as part of an overall supply chain optimization (SCO) effort. Initial studies have indicated that moving away from brand-specific sourcing, procurement, and other supply chain-related activities toward centralized, corporation-wide processes and technology will result in significant cost savings and a relatively short payback period for the investments made.

In this case, you *must* consider the strategic sourcing initiative as part of the roadmap effort. Or, stated another way: at least when it comes to supply chain-related data (e.g., a Vendor master), reporting and analytics, and other facets of the corporation's SCM systems, you *cannot* treat these systems, data, and processes independently for purposes of scaling and scoping the enterprise for the upcoming roadmap.

3.3 LEAN MANUFACTURING

Companies embark on *lean manufacturing* initiatives to optimize the time and resources that go into their respective manufacturing processes while also pursuing quality improvement, with "value preservation" always top of mind. Data management is an important contributor to lean initiatives:

> Across the industry, Supply Chain teams are shaping change by driving Lean principles through our data management and purchasing systems. Similar to the impact of reducing physical steps in the manufacturing process, removal of unnecessary data transfers, entry, and validation yields important benefits both internally and externally. Fewer data management points significantly decreases the opportunities for errors (and their associated costs) as well as reducing the processing steps that need monitoring. The greater the complexity of the businesses supported, the greater the need for Lean business processes. (Johnson, 2013)

A lean manufacturing initiative needs to be factored into a company's EDM roadmap to clearly understand what is required of the organization's data to support the lean effort.

3.4 "MEGA-PROCESSES"

Companies and governmental agencies have paid attention to business process efficiencies and effectiveness for years, dating back to the Scientific Management days of Frederick Taylor in the early 1900s and continuing through "movements" such as Business Process Reengineering (BPR) and Business Process Management (BPM). Increasingly, organizations are focusing efforts on what might be called "mega-processes" – i.e., those that transcend a given department's boundaries and which have sweeping impacts across a large portion of an organization. Common "mega-processes" include:

- Order to cash
- Quote to cash
- Quote to order
- Purchase to pay
- Procure to pay

These "mega-processes" require significant data interchange and flow among the various components, with speed and accuracy of paramount importance. "Data barriers" such as manual data entry and spreadsheet-driven data interchange are deadly to the objectives of these "mega-processes" and need to be addressed. Therefore, any such initiatives must also factor into the EDM roadmap.

3.5 HEIGHTENED RISK MITIGATION AND MANAGEMENT

Companies are increasingly concerned about risk. Major consultancies have very large practices devoted to business risk (BR) and technical risk (TR), with a seemingly endless flow of work coming from clients in all industries and across the world.

To understand and then mitigate risk, you need significant amounts of "the right" data, and EDM programs are often closely aligned with risk management efforts. For example, a product manager at Eagle Investment Systems noted in an October, 2013 report:

The first driver is the continued underlying need to improve data quality for key initiatives such as risk management and exposure reporting. The deeper investment managers can drill into their portfolios, the better they understand their direct and indirect exposure to various investments, which strengthens risk management at the firm and helps enable better business decisions.

> *Increasingly, data management is at the core of everything investment managers are doing, from accounting to performance measurement and reporting. Centralized data management creates tremendous efficiencies and allows multiple systems to directly integrate with and use the same set of data. Another driver of EDM adoption is industry regulation such as the DoddFrank Act and Solvency II, which push companies to increase the types of data that they support and the frequency at which the data is required. (Incisive, 2013)*

As with the other business initiatives discussed in this chapter, risk management efforts need to be closely aligned with your EDM roadmap.

3.6 ENTERPRISE SYSTEMS INITIATIVES

In the beginning of Chapter 2 we looked at a fictional "Company #1" – a large health club operator – in which its core business operations are run on a single suite of enterprise systems (ERP, CRM, etc.).

Very often, though, companies will find themselves with a complex federation of enterprise systems:

- Multiple ERP packages, perhaps from different vendors (e.g., SAP, Oracle) or maybe with multiple packages from the same vendor but which feature radically different customizations for different business units;

- Multiple CRM systems that rely on a complex patchwork of point-to-point data exchanges to support cross-brand customer loyalty programs or similar customer-facing programs;
- Multiple supply chain packages aligned with specific brands and/or geographies (as discussed earlier in this chapter)

Very often, EDM roadmaps find themselves alongside a parallel path that will, if successful, change the landscape of an organization's enterprise systems. Three very common situations are:

- New ERP implementation
- Enterprise systems migration
- Enterprise systems rationalization

3.6.1 New ERP Implementation

Strategists, data architects, and others who have spent the majority of their career working in large companies or government agencies are often surprised to learn that many sizable companies are still largely run on spreadsheets, with little or no enterprise systems software present.

Consider a company that has reached several hundred million dollars (U.S.) of annual revenue but runs its back office largely on PC-based accounting software; i.e., "ERP light." Payroll is outsourced; supply chain, customer management, and other core business functions are handled through a variety of custom-developed one-by-one systems as well as spreadsheet-driven manual workflows.

Company executives have decided that the next wave of growth requires greater economies of scale and attention to workflow quality than can be achieved by perpetuating the systems status quo, and the company's first ERP system will be implemented.

In this case, the EDM roadmap needs to consider the impacts of the ERP implementation: what master data sets need to be created that don't currently exist, for example, or how operational reporting issues that people grudgingly put up will be improved as part of the ERP effort. As described earlier in this chapter, some EDM-related improvements to the current state may already be part of the ERP project; in other situations, the ERP team may not yet have given adequate attention to the problematic state of Customer, Product, Vendor, and other key master data subjects.

Either way, the EDM roadmap must be "ERP aware" if a new implementation is underway or is expected soon to be.

3.6.2 Enterprise Systems Migration

Other organizations may already have ERP, CRM, SCM, HCM, and other systems in place, but for a variety of reasons the current packages have been deemed inadequate, and a one-for-one swap is forthcoming. For example, the company may run on an on-premises integrated package of ERP, CRM, HCM, etc. but due to cost and support, sunsetted vendor software, or other reasons they are in the process of moving to a cloud-hosted integrated software suite.

From data quality to master data to data interchanges, all aspects of the newly hosted enterprise systems' data landscape need to be factored into the EDM roadmap.

3.6.3 Enterprise Systems Rationalization and Consolidation

Consider the complex federation of multiple ERP and CRM systems across multiple brands and geographies, as described earlier in this section. An organization may grudgingly come to the conclusion that its overall structure, culture, and business model is not suitable for migration of all of these disparate systems into a single consolidated, enterprise-wide platform...yet today's "total mess" is unsustainable. At the very least, some degree of *enterprise systems rationalization* needs to occur.

As with the previous two enterprise systems-related initiatives (new ERP; one-for-one migration), rationalization efforts need to be factored into the EDM roadmap.

3.7 ENTERPRISE-LEVEL BUSINESS QUALITY INITIATIVES

Business quality initiatives such as Total Quality Management (TQM) and Six Sigma make extensive use of data to monitor, measure, and report results. The broader any one of these types of initiatives reaches with regards to organizational scope, the greater the need for enterprise-scale data management, with particular emphasis on data quality and uniformity.

Systems and applications being implemented to support TQM, Six Sigma, or some other type of business quality initiative need to be considered alongside the EDM roadmap, the same as the other business initiatives discussed throughout this chapter.

3.8 CHAPTER SUMMARY

The key takeaway from this chapter is that you not only need to assess *today's* current state of EDM (Chapter 2) but also be cognizant of the trajectory of enterprise data – both positive and negative – that will result from key business initiatives and how well (or not) they are addressing EDM "hot spots."

If a particular initiative is underway and part of the activity is to "clean up the Product and Customer master data across the enterprise" then that body of work must be accounted for as you determine the roadmap and various milestones. You will still need to determine if the results from, for example, the implementation of a new, enterprise-wide Product Information Management System (PIMS) as part of cross-brand strategic sourcing is well aligned with what the future EDM state should be, or if additional work may need to occur. But addressing a current "product master mess" while disregarding the fact that "mess" is being addressed is the type of occurrence that can severely undermine an EDM initiative.

REFERENCES

Johnson, S., 2013. "Expanding the Relevance of Lean Manufacturing to Data". Manufacturing Transformation Blog. http://www.apriso.com/blog/2013/08/the-continued-relevance-of-lean-manufacturing-2/.

Incisive Media, 2013. "Inside Reference Data, suppl. Special Report: Enterprise Data Management". October, pp. 8–15.

CHAPTER 4

Surveying Relevant Enterprise Data Management Technologies

4.1 INTRODUCTION

The title of a 2007 article said it best, even before "Big Data" burst onto the scene (Reagan and Rowlands, 2007):

Key Technologies Enabling a Seismic Shift in Enterprise Data Management

Strategists and architects chartered with guiding their organizations' respective enterprise data management capabilities need to be fully aware that even beyond data-related products and their capabilities, core technologies continue to evolve on a regular basis. Some of this evolution is...well, evolutionary; i.e., a regular and orderly expansion and enhancement of capabilities over a number of years. Other changes, though, are disruptive and bring about the aforementioned seismic shifts, either individually or in tandem with others.

This chapter presents a high-level survey of the key categories of technologies most relevant to an enterprise data management initiative and the roadmap to reach a planned future state. Whereas the products and their respective features will no doubt continue to evolve, and as new disruptive technologies (think the Internet, mobile computing, Big Data, etc.) further expand "the art of the possible," the overall categories presented in this chapter will be a good working model for the foreseeable future.

4.2 DATABASES AND DATA STORAGE

A bit of background in the evolution and history of database management systems (DBMSs) is helpful to understand today's – and tomorrow's – data storage and management capabilities.

In the early days of computing, data was managed primarily through files: initially on punched card decks and magnetic tapes, and then on "direct access storage devices" – DASD, or disks. Various file systems such as IBM's ISAM and VSAM allowed indexed access to individual records, greatly expanding the repertoire of application developers with regards to data management. Still, most file systems lacked capabilities for security, transaction management semantics, and support for multiple users and applications.

Beginning in the 1960s and throughout the 1970s, software and systems vendors began introducing *databases* as an alternative to "flat file" systems. Many different structural models came onto the scenes, with most of them supporting relationships among data via physical pointers.

By the late 1980s, database technology had largely evolved to a common industry model based on *relational database management systems* (RDBMSs)...the table/row/column, spreadsheet-like paradigm that most IT professionals know and use today. Throughout the 1980s, although, relational database technology was still maturing to the point where RDBMSs could confidently be used for mission-critical applications in banking, retail, government, and other industries and sectors. Until that maturity occurred, however, older-style DBMSs such as IBM's IMS, Cullinet's IDMS, and others continued to be used along with file systems for many critical applications and their storage needs.

In the early 1990s when data warehousing came onto the scene, strategists and architects were faced with a quandary: where to store the consolidated, synthesized data that would feed into the business intelligence (BI) tools to present users with the timely, high-value insights they were after? Specifically, the quandary was this: it had taken almost an entire decade before RDBMSs were "ready for prime time" to provide acceptable performance for transactional applications, but data warehousing was designed to support different database design techniques than for transactional systems (dimensional vs. normalized).

Consequently, the early 1990s saw different types of specialized databases and data storage engines come to market to support BI and data warehousing. Vendors such as Red Brick Systems adapted the relational model to perform well with dimensionally structured data, while other vendors such as IRI and Arbor Software developed and marketed *multidimensional database engines* (Express and Essbase, respectively). Thus, it was commonplace to find organizations with their transactional systems running on top of RDBMSs such as Oracle, Sybase, DB2, and others, with data regularly fed into data warehouses and data marts running on specialized DBMSs.

By the late 1990s and into the early 2000s, however, RDBMS vendors focused significant attention on evolving their products to be able to satisfy analytical needs (e.g., Online Analytical Processing – OLAP) equally as well as transactional needs. Relational products were extended to support star-joins, bitmapped indexes, and other mechanisms suitable for dimensional analysis and other BI needs. Massively parallel processing (MPP) technology further enhanced the capacity and performance of RDBMSs. By the mid-2000s, data warehouse strategists and architects had largely settled on RDBMSs as their primary data warehousing platforms, with specialized structures such as analytical cubes used as part of an RDBMS-centric architecture.

By the mid- and late 2000s, however, the data volumes required to be managed by data warehouses were beginning to put significant strain on the RDBMS platforms. While early generation data warehouses typically stored summarized data rather than lowest-grain transactional data, modern data warehouses increasingly included the most detailed transactions as well as higher-level summarizations. While RDBMS and storage technology were certainly capable of storing significantly larger volumes than in earlier years, capacity demands were quickly catching up with and threatening to surpass what the RDBMS engines could comfortably manage.

As a result, *data warehousing appliances* – specialized high-capacity, high-performance engines intended *only* for data warehousing rather than general-purpose database management – reached the market. Vendors such as Netezza, DATAllegro, Greenplum, and others began to swing the pendulum back to the landscape of the early and mid-1990s with "real" data warehousing taking place at least in part on specialized databases rather than general-purpose RDBMSs. Major DBMS vendors either made acquisitions to broaden their data management offerings (e.g., IBM purchased Netezza; Microsoft purchased DATAllegro) or brought their own specialized DW appliances to market.

Another family of "sort of DW appliances" is that of columnar databases such as Vertica and ParAccel that store their data in a manner conducive to serving up large volumes of data to answer certain types of business questions.

Then we have the Big Data revolution in which previously unconceivable volumes of increasingly complex data are stored outside of the relational realm, and in which names such as Hadoop, MongoDB, Splunk, and others have become increasingly commonplace in an organization's data landscape.

So what's the significance of the brief history presented above? Simply this: in today's and tomorrow's enterprise data landscape, *all* of the following data management and storage engines will almost certainly be present:

- Traditional RDBMSs
- Analytic cubes (the "descendants" of multidimensional databases such as Express and Essbase)
- Specialized DBMSs such as columnar databases
- Big data engines

Therefore, EDM strategists and architects need to have an overall familiarity with *each* of these data management product categories and, most importantly, their respective strengths and weaknesses. Unlike the brief period in the early and mid-2000s when data management had gravitated toward multipurpose RDBMSs, today's and tomorrow's environments will likely be component-based with a variety of different engines and models used for different transactional, reporting, and advanced analytical purposes.

On the other hand, it's always a possibility that the current "specialization divergence" in data management engines could once again coalesce around a new generation of relationally based, multipurpose DBMSs, reprising what occurred in the late 1990s and early 2000s. Seismic shifts in data management technology (referring back to the quote that opened this chapter) are nothing new. In 1995, I wrote a book that looked at the direction of database technology over the next 5 years (Simon, 1995). While many of the forecasts proved to be accurate, others were not due to significantly disruptive technologies such as the Internet and other factors such as the then-murky Y2K problem. Thus, today's drive back toward data management specialization could once again reverse course; only time will tell.

4.3 DATABASE ADMINISTRATION AND MAINTENANCE

Every data store across the enterprise needs to be backed up; recovered if necessary; monitored for performance and security issues; and undergo all of the other traditional administration and maintenance functions. Typically, these functions – and the tools through which to perform those tasks – reside in the realm of the database and systems administration professionals. Still, EDM strategists and architects should at least be aware of the newest generations of technologies for these functions, particularly those that are *not* closely coupled with a particular DBMS but rather might span products from multiple vendors. Key enterprise data management critical success factors (CSFs) such as availability, performance and response time, and security are often instantiated through these administration and maintenance tools, so even if their operations will be delegated to DBAs and systems administrators, they do fit into the overall EDM technology landscape.

4.4 DATA VIRTUALIZATION

Chapter 1 looked at the failure of distributed database management systems (DDBMSs) in the early 1990s and the resulting shift toward first-generation data warehousing as a means to address the ever-growing problem of fragmented data silos. The material in Chapter 1 also mentioned that beyond data warehousing, another school of thought was to repurpose the read-write DDBMSs as read-only engines with a synthesized data model managed by an abstraction layer that provided location and platform transparency on top of multiple underlying databases. Further, this read-only DDBMS approach has ebbed and flowed since the early 1990s, experiencing periodic interest and excitement under labels such as *virtual data warehousing* and *enterprise information integration (EII)*...and today, *data virtualization*.

An enterprise data management architecture may well contain data virtualization capabilities from non-DBMS vendors such as Composite Software and Informatica, or from leading vendors such as IBM.

Even with today's core technologies being far superior to those of prior generations in which data virtualization saw a spike in popularity, strategists and architects want to still be cautious about the roles for this paradigm in an overall enterprise data management landscape. Certain use cases are well suited to data virtualization, while other scenarios are still better left toward more traditional data warehousing/data mart approaches...or perhaps newer Big Data technology. Still, data virtualization is likely to play at least a specialized role in the EDM roadmap of many organizations.

4.5 MASTER DATA MANAGEMENT

Master data management (MDM) is a broad-sweeping term that means different things to various individuals. To some, MDM is an all-encompassing discipline that can only succeed if all transactional and reporting/analytic systems agree on uniform definitions and business rules for key subject areas such as Customer, Product, Vendor, Order, Employee, and so on. Absent 100% agreement, MDM will be a failure and chaos will reign.

Others take a more pragmatic approach to MDM, with a dual-faceted philosophy of:

- Uniformity when possible and prudent, but also...
- "Agreeing to disagree" over certain subject areas as an acceptable outcome, but with the variations precisely defined and documented

Some see MDM as applying primarily to the always-critical Customer and Product areas, with specialized software being used to manage Customer Data Integration (CDI) and Product Information Management (PIM). Others see MDM as squarely within the operational control of the enterprise's ERP systems...or, ideally, as the epicenter of an integrated single-vendor suite of ERP, CRM, SCM, HCM, and other key enterprise applications.

Regardless of philosophy, terminology, specialized software, or answers to "who owns master data" one point is abundantly clear: MDM *must* receive significant attention throughout an EDM roadmap initiative. Technologies will change, as MDM capabilities continue to come to market and products from leading independent vendors, DBMS vendors, and others continue to be enhanced. But without fail, MDM needs to be an important part of the technology portfolio supporting EDM.

4.6 METADATA MANAGEMENT

Metadata management has been an on-again, off-again topic of interest since the mid- to late 1970s. The concept of "data about data" managed through some form of a *data dictionary* was initially attractive in the days when programming languages, early DBMSs, operating systems, and rudimentary querying and reporting tools almost always mandated cryptic, highly compressed naming conventions. To assist users in understanding that, for example, "GRPL1" meant "Gross Revenue for Product Line 1" and "GRPL2" referred to "Gross Revenue for Product Line 2," the plain language data dictionaries could be consulted to guide both systems professionals and end users alike.

In the 1980s when Computer-Aided Software Engineering (CASE) tools began to gain in popularity, *repositories* of metadata were often used to consolidate and coordinate definitions from various types of tools: data modeling, process modeling, structured software design, etc. Plain language definitions for cryptic terms was still of great importance, but so was the capture of management of semantic information about the data elements and software components being designed…as well as what the linkages were among those elements and components. One of the key objectives of multitool metadata management was to enable *impact analysis* at the cross-component level: i.e., "if we change the definition of this particular column in the database, what are all the programs and other systems that will be impacted and which we will need to modify?"

As data warehousing and BI took hold throughout the 1990s, metadata became increasingly important for both BI reporting products as well as extraction, transformation, and loading (ETL) tools. Now, a dichotomy began to emerge in the world of metadata, with two distinct and often disjoint purposes in play:

- *user-facing metadata* was typically aligned with the BI tools to provide descriptive information and clarity of business rules about the structure and content of reports (i.e., "what does this report column contain?" and "what does this number really mean?" types of questions);

- *system-facing metadata* captured and managed the details of ETL runs: how many rows of data were read from a given source file; how many rows failed various quality assurance checks; how many rows were written into the target data warehouse or data mart; how long did the ETL job take; and so on.

Visionary architects and developers often attempted to link user-facing and system-facing metadata together to provide insights into *data lineage* – i.e., not only what a particular number in a report meant, but when the underlying data that was showing up on the report was last refreshed in the data warehouse and the source(s) that provided that data. Most early attempts at end-to-end data lineage were cobbled together and often mothballed before too long.

Today, metadata management across the enterprise data management landscape might be viewed as an immutable capability that cannot be overlooked. Every type of data-oriented product produces at least rudimentary metadata, even if the metadata might only be regular updates to some type of logging file. Design-level tools all provide fields for data modelers, report designers and developers, and others to enter as much descriptive information as desired. (Whether those individuals actually do make those entries, and then keep them up to date, is another matter.)

Metadata management is a necessity in the realm of enterprise data management, especially given the breadth and depth of the data that needs to be managed across the typical enterprise and the portfolio of tools required to accomplish that management.

4.7 DATA QUALITY AND PROFILING

One of the most-cited mantras of the early days of computing was *GIGO*: "garbage in, garbage out." Essentially, if "bad data" made its way into a system, overall results would likely be erroneous regardless of how well-designed a given software program might be.

Software developers are taught how to filter incoming data via user-entry forms, application-to-application interfaces, external bulk data feeds, and other intake mechanisms to prevent errors from making their way into an application. Modern databases can be designed with DBMS-managed constraints to control ranges and lists of permissible values and cross-table referential integrity.

Still, problematic data remains…well, a problem.

The very nature of modern enterprise data management means that inevitably, data will regularly flow from one component to another. *At every single instance of data interchange, errors that didn't previously exist may be introduced.* This means that even if a company's or governmental agency's application software developers had done a 100% perfect job in filtering out erroneous data from user entry screens and inbound bulk data feeds, *within* the enterprise errors could be introduced at any time as data flows from one environment to another.

Various techniques fall under the umbrella of "data quality" including:

• *Data profiling*: From one-time analysis-phase scans to regularly repeated quality assurance-driven scans, data in a given system is reviewed analyzed to understand the structure, content, implicit and/ or explicit business rules, and other facets. The primary objective of data profiling is deep understanding of and insight into the details of a given collection of data…not just whether data is "good" or "bad" but for given fields the ranges of values or lists of values; referential integrity constraints; business rules; temporal properties (how the state of a given data element in a particular data store may change over time); and so on.

• *Data cleansing*: Outright errors and anomalies are either fixed or removed…the intention being to improve the overall quality of data and thus its business value. Data cleansing may occur "in place" – i.e., as part of the overall profiling process, fixing discovered errors – or as part of a data interchange process (e.g., ETL) as data flows from one database to another.

Regardless of the current state of a given organization's data quality (see Chapter 2), *sustainable* improvement should be a key aspect to any EDM effort. Further, a philosophy of *eternal vigilance* should hallmark the effort; i.e., as quality improvements occur, data stewards and others ardently, almost fanatically guard against "backsliding" even as new systems come on line and new interfaces are developed.

A relatively recent school of thought is that data profiling, data cleansing, and other quality metrics can be infused into the realm of Big Data to take advantage of very fast processors and ultra-large overall storage capacity. Regardless of the exact mechanisms a given organization chooses to implement data quality, doing so as part of an EDM effort must be a given.

4.8 DATA GOVERNANCE

Some vendors bundle some of the above-mentioned capabilities into an overall *data governance* product framework. Informatica, for example, describes their data governance product at the time of writing as including (Informatica, 2014):

- data discovery and profiling
- data lineage and proactive data quality monitoring
- MDM
- metadata management
- business glossary
- data retention and archiving

Similarly, Collibra lists a business semantics glossary, data stewardship manager, and reference data accelerator as part of its data governance center (Collibra, 2014).

4.9 DATA INTERCHANGE AND MOVEMENT

Since the dawn of the data warehousing era, the *ETL* of data from source systems into data warehouses/data marts have been an integral part of EDM architectures. Initially the ETL process was largely accomplished via custom-written SQL code...a practice which still exists today in many organizations, at least in part. As early-generation ETL products from vendors such as Prism Solutions and Evolutionary Technologies gave way to longer-standing products such as Informatica's PowerCenter, DataStage, and SQL Server Integration Services (SSIS), ETL tools have become an integral part of most EDM landscapes.

But ETL is not the only mechanism for interchanging data among EDM systems and components. Other models include:

- *DBMS-driven replication services*: The DBMSs themselves contain the means for replicating, or copying in an orderly manner, data across multiple database instances.
- *Third-party replication services*: Non-DBMS vendors such as Attunity, Informatica, and Sybase (SAP) manage the data replication process in a landscape that may (but doesn't necessarily have to) include heterogeneous databases.
- *Web services-based data exchange*: Many organizations build a foundation based on *service-oriented architecture (SOA)* concepts and technology to move data among systems and components.
- *Bulk load services*: Still other data acquisition occurs when large volumes of source data are transferred – typically into a data warehouse – from internal or external data providers. Various "fast load" techniques are used to "ingest" the data, and the ingestion may occur on either a one-time or repeating basis.

The modern enterprise data management environment will likely contain multiple mechanisms by which data interchange and movement occurs, with a variety of products used in various places. EDM strategists and architects need to not only decide which products to use, but also to be aware of architectural models and paradigms for integration and data flows.

For example, conventional wisdom since data warehousing came onto the scene is that most data cleansing, filtering, and transformation should occur *before* data arrives in the data warehousing environment, and that designers and developers needed to be very selective as to what data was actually made available for reporting and analysis. With the advent of Big Data technology and paradigms, an increasing school of thought is that "most or all" of the enterprise's data should be ingested into a Big Data engine and *then* the data quality and data transformations can be put to work using the superior power of the Big Data environment.

Regardless of how that conventional wisdom may or may not change in the future, those charged with building a roadmap to a robust, sustainable EDM environment need to be aware of various forms of data movement products and their respective capabilities, along with the data flow patterns those tools will fit over time.

4.10 DATA RETRIEVAL, PREPARATION, AND DELIVERY (BUSINESS INTELLIGENCE, REPORTING, AND ANALYTICS)

Note that this section header uses general language for its main body, with specific categories – business intelligence, reporting, and analytics – included in parentheses.

The data management landscape has long been hallmarked by "wars" over alternative approaches or categorizations:

- Multidimensional Online Analytical Processing (MOLAP) versus Relational Online Analytical Processing (ROLAP) in the 1990s
- The Inmon versus Kimball architectural approaches to enterprise-scale data warehousing in the 2000s
- What constitutes a "data warehouse" versus a "data mart"

An interesting "battle," albeit a less dogmatic one than those mentioned above, is being waged today as Big Data technologies and operating models move more into the mainstream of enterprise data management. Specifically: what is the difference, if any, between *business intelligence* and *analytics*?

Over the years, any number of taxonomies have been offered by vendors, consultants, and analysts in an attempt to categorize and provide demarcations among different classes, look-and-feel paradigms, and capabilities of user-facing tools that deliver data and information. For example, in Simon (1997) this author presented a categorization of BI as follows:

- *Basic Reporting and Querying*: Early and mid-1990s-era reporting and querying tools primarily delivered static or lightly parameterized reports, with the reports themselves as the end points (i.e., no further drilling-down or drilling-up, pivoting, etc.)
- *Online Analytical Processing*: First-generation products that were categorized as "BI" typically took the reporting model a step further to include the aforementioned drilling-down, drilling-up, and other "slicing and dicing" online functionality that didn't require the running of an entirely new report.
- *Data Mining*: Although many technologists in the mid-1990s considered data mining to be a separate discipline than BI, this author's perspective was that most forms of discovery-oriented, model-driven data analysis – including what has become widely

known today as *predictive analytics* – was in fact a subset of the overall BI continuum, providing "tell me what is likely to happen" and "tell me something interesting and important" types of insights.

- *Executive Information Systems*: The evolution of 1980s-era *executive information systems* focused on key executive-level insights delivered through early-generation dashboards, "briefing books," and other highly condensed screens and printouts.

The key point to the above taxonomy is that multiple types of data retrieval, preparation, and delivery were *all* included in the overall category of *business intelligence*, meaning that a holistic collection of well-architected data should exist to serve *all* of those paradigms.

Flash-forward to the mid-late 2000s and the mainstreaming of data mining…particularly as presented in works such as Davenport and Harris (2007), Siegel (2013), and Silver (2012) that advocate the value of predictive analytics and other forms of data mining as the next wave of driving insights out of data. Little or no mention is made of traditional reporting/querying or OLAP in these works. Consequently, a dichotomy has developed into the mid-2010s where many see *analytics* (or "advanced analytics" or "predictive analytics" or some other semantic variation) as a different discipline than *business intelligence*. Or, stated another way: in the view of some, BI (and by extension, data warehousing) are tired disciplines that have rarely lived up to the promise of actionable insights, whereas the modern era of Big Data coupled with predictive analytics far surpasses the BI/data warehousing generation in terms of business value.

In this author's opinion, and leaving aside semantics and terminology for a moment, the Big Data/predictive analytics/data discovery paradigm is the latest incarnation of the data mining segment in the aforementioned 1997 BI taxonomy. But whereas we've seen tremendous advances in managing ultra-large data sets and building predictive models, we've also seen significant enhancements to the reporting/OLAP family of products, as well as dashboards and other executive-style delivery paradigms. In other words, *all* of the categories have seen vastly improved products and enabling core technologies over the years, and no category actually supplants another in the overall BI continuum.

Finally, with regards to semantics and terminology, blogger Timo Elliott states that "What's the difference between Business Analytics and Business Intelligence? The correct answer is: everybody has an opinion, but nobody knows, and you shouldn't care." (Elliott, 2011)...an opinion shared by this author. Elliott notes that vendors such as SAS, SAP, and others all tailor definitions of these terms to their various product lineups, meaning that an apples-to-apples comparison of even what two vendors (or analysts or consultancies or academics) mean by "business analytics" or "BI" or "advanced analytics" is all but impossible.

Therefore, the category that EDM strategists and architects must carefully follow with regards to their respective roadmaps might be better generalized as (per the title of this section) data retrieval, preparation, and delivery:

- *Data retrieval*: The first-line extraction (whether physical copying or in-place access) of the relevant data required that will eventually deliver a specific insight to an end user or other application;
- *Data preparation*: Whatever filtering, cleansing, aggregation, transformations, or other functions are required to turn "raw" data into a form ready for delivery; and
- *Data delivery*: The transmission and placement of data to desktop or laptop computer reports, mobile device-based app or browser screens, text alerts, or whatever consumption methods are used by a given user or application.

No matter how solid an enterprise data management architecture might be, shortcomings in the user-facing side of retrieving, preparing, and delivering data to users and applications will severely compromise the overall business value of the EDM environment. Core technology and interaction paradigms will continue to march forward; vendors, consultants, and analysts will continue to offer new taxonomies and categorizations, not to mention terminology; and the user-facing landscape in 2020 will no doubt look at least a little bit different than today's, just as today's looks different than that of the 2000s and certainly the 1990s.

4.11 OTHER CORE AND ENABLING TECHNOLOGIES

Beyond the various categories of EDM-related technologies described thus far in this chapter, strategists and architects need to also consider:

- *Mobile technologies*: The shift from PCs to mobile devices continues to accelerate, and while it's questionable if PCs will truly disappear anytime in the next decade, it's a given that mobile-based data delivery will become an increasingly larger portion of any given enterprise's landscape year after year.

- *Web "X. Y" technologies and architectures* – In 2004, an O'Reilly Media conference popularized the concept of *Web 2.0* as the next generation of Internet-based technologies and paradigms (Graham, 2005). More recently, articles and papers have begun appearing that discuss the concept of *Web 3.0*. As time marches forward, it's inevitable that consultants, analysts, vendors, and academics will continue to periodically propose next-generation "Web X.Y" concepts, technologies, and architectures...each of which will continue to play an important role in enterprise data management.
- *Wearable technologies*: From Google Glass (Google, 2014) to "smart clothing" to other new innovations we will see over the next decade, EDM architecture needs to be "wearable device aware" with regards to both data collection and data delivery.
- *Voice recognition and natural language processing*: Millions of phone and tablet users were introduced to voice recognition technology in 2011, courtesy of Apple Computer's iPhone 4S and Siri. Computer scientists have pursued the incorporation of voice technologies into computing devices dating back to the 1950s, when Bell Laboratories introduced its "Audrey" system that recognized spoken digits (Pinolla, 2011).

Likewise, throughout the 1980s leading computing companies heavily focused on the development of *5th Generation Languages* (5GLs) in which query-oriented – but still syntactically bound – 4th Generation Languages would be "unshackled" and natural language interfaces to software would become commonplace. Siri and similar technology helped bring together voice recognition technology and natural language processing, and going forward EDM environments will increasingly see the data retrieval, preparation, and delivery function (discussed in the previous section) managed through Siri-like interfaces.

- *Workflow and collaboration*: Attempts have been made over the years to couple traditional BI with workflow and collaboration engines, with varying degrees of success (or lack thereof). Increasingly, BI will be workflow-enabled to prevent "lost in the shuffle" situations where critical insights are produced but for one reason or another, never acted upon. We will also see increasingly complex analytical processing that require collaboration from multiple individuals and/ or automated systems. Consequently, workflow- and collaboration-enablement of enterprise data will likely become commonplace in robust, world-class EDM architectures.

- *Enterprise security*: Barely a day goes by without a story about credit card numbers, social security numbers, or private health care data being stolen or otherwise compromised. EDM architectures must contain top-to-bottom, end-to-end security that encompasses *all* data stores, data flows, data access…everything.

4.12 STAYING ON TOP OF PROLIFERATING TECHNOLOGIES

Beyond the usual methods to keep abreast of changes in technologies – going to conferences; scanning or following dozens of blogs, periodicals, and other online content; participating in online-targeted interest discussions (e.g., via LinkedIn Groups); etc. – the strategists and architects within any organization should pool their efforts to collectively keep themselves as informed as possible.

One approach is for the collection of individuals involved in an organization's enterprise data management efforts to divide up the categories mentioned in this chapter where:

- each individual "majors" in a given category; and also
- "minors" in one or two others.

Some of the categories that are very broad – databases and reporting/ analytic tools in particular – can be further subdivided. For example, one individual might "major" in relational DBMS technology (or a particular RDBMS product if there is an immutable organizational standard), while someone else might focus on Big Data and a third person "major" in multidimensional technology for analytical usage.

The objective is to gain as much cross-coverage as possible to enable EDM leaders to perform whatever primary job functions are assigned to them at the moment while still each spending a small but steady portion of his or her time attending conferences and seminars, reading, etc. By making this a formal part of each EDM leader's job, the collective time spent on "R&D" style activities will add up to a meaningful amount, to the benefit of the organization and its EDM efforts.

REFERENCES

Collibra Data Governance Center, https://www.collibra.com/data-governance-center/.

Davenport, T.H., Harris, J.G., 2007. Competing on Analytics: The New Science of Winning. Harvard Business Review Press.

Elliott, T., 2011. "Business Analytics vs. Business Intelligence?". *Business Analytics* blog, http://timoelliott.com/blog/2011/03/business-analytics-vs-business-intelligence.html.

Google Glass splash page, http://www.google.com/glass/start/what-it-does/.

Graham, P., "Web 2.0." http://www.paulgraham.com/web20.html.

Informatica Data Governance Solution. http://www.informatica.com/us/solutions/enterprise-data-integration-and-management/data-governance/.

"History of voice recognition: from Audrey to Siri". itBusiness.ca, November 4, 2011. http://www.itbusiness.ca/news/history-of-voice-recognition-from-audrey-to-siri/15008.

Reagan, J., Rowlands, I., 2007. Key technologies enabling a seismic shift in enterprise data management. Business Intelligence J. 12.1, First Quarter.

Siegel, E., 2013. Predictive Analytics: The Power to Predict Who Will Click, Buy, Lie, or Die. Wiley.

Silver, N., 2012. The Signal and the Noise: Why So Many Predictions Fail-but Some Don't. The Penguin Press.

Simon, A., 1995. Strategic Database Technology: Management for the Year 2000. Morgan Kaufmann Publishers.

Simon, A., 1997. Data Warehousing for Dummies. HungryMinds.

CHAPTER 5

Building an Enterprise Data Management and Business Intelligence Roadmap

5.1 INTRODUCTION

The enterprise data management (EDM) roadmap effort actually begins with the body of work discussed in Chapters 2 and 3: assessing the current state as well as surveying key business initiatives that are "EDM-sensitive."

Ideally, the activities described in those two chapters will occur in a very rapid manner, taking only 2 or 3 weeks at most for even the largest enterprise. Upon completion of those prerequisite activities, the heart of the roadmap effort can then begin.

5.2 BEFORE PROCEEDING: PREREQUISITES FOR A SUCCESSFUL ENTERPRISE DATA MANAGEMENT ROADMAP EFFORT

Many readers may have been part of a roadmap-type effort – for EDM or perhaps another technology discipline – that concluded in, at best, lackluster results. Perhaps the final deliverables turned into "shelfware" that never again saw the light of day past the final presentation. Or maybe the future state architecture and the roadmap phases looked as if they had been lifted from a textbook or collection of white papers, filled with all of the latest buzzwords but with very little "grounding in the reality" of the organization and its business processes.

Still other roadmap efforts turn out, in retrospect, to have zero sponsorship beyond the Director-level individual with a modest budget who cobbled together a team as inexpensively as he or she could…but quite literally, nobody with any significant authority in the enterprise cares about the results (or may even be aware that the effort actually took place!). Sometimes work on an EDM roadmap takes place only as an "additional duty" on the part of several individuals, all of whom devote a couple of hours here and there but otherwise have their regular jobs and responsibilities demanding the majority of their time.

Before beginning the core of the EDM roadmap effort, a number of prerequisites need to be in place to avoid the aforementioned dead-end outcomes. Specifically:

- *Team composition*: An experienced team of professionals, broadly skilled in the myriad of EDM-related topics covered in Chapter 4, needs to be in place. For a smaller-scale effort, one or two individuals may be sufficient; while for a larger-scale, longer-term effort, the team may require four or five individuals. Regardless of the actual number of team members, they need to have previously delivered EDM roadmap engagements. Further, these individuals need to either be engaged for the roadmap effort on a full-time basis or, if part-time, with an immutable portion of their work time carved out for roadmap-related work.
- *A dogma-free philosophy*: The roadmap engagement itself and those who deliver the body of work need to have a dispassionate, objective view about EDM architecture, core technologies, the organizational structure and culture…everything. Too many EDM-related efforts are compromised by preconceived notions and dogmatic thinking on the part of the engagement team or perhaps the sponsors.
- *Defined rules of engagement*: A RACI (Responsible/Accountable/Consulted/Informed) or equivalent matrix needs to be put in place with all interested parties and what their RACI-driven roles are for each phase and activity of the effort. The rules of engagement need to be agreed to before the engagement begins to prevent politics-driven and other problems once the effort is underway.
- *Genuine CxO leadership*: The all-too-common mantra of "we need leadership from the organization's executives for this effort" needs to be a reality for an EDM initiative. From the kickoff meeting to regular status meetings to the final readout, the COO, CFO, and even the CEO need to be universally seen by all as intensely interested and vested in the outcome of the effort and the build-out of the roadmap that is produced.
- *Adequate time*: For a smaller-scale enterprise (see Chapter 2), a minimum of 8–9 weeks is required to thoroughly accomplish the

body of work required for a well-thought-out EDM roadmap. For a broader, more complex enterprise, engagements may run anywhere from 20 to 30 weeks.

5.3 THE EDM ROADMAP ENGAGEMENT

Even if every member of the roadmap team is an internal employee rather than outside consultants, the effort should be treated as if it were a consulting engagement, with:

- Formally scheduled beginning and ending dates
- Officially assigned resources with the variety of skills and experience levels needed to successfully deliver the roadmap
- A formal budget
- An official engagement kickoff meeting
- Status reports, checkpoints at key milestones, deliverable review cycles, and other project-type best practices
- A mid-engagement "Stakeholders' Summit" (described later in this chapter) to establish a "consensus beachhead" from which the remainder of the engagement can then proceed
- An end-of-engagement readout of the final deliverables, with an immediate call to action from the CxO ranks

One can find many different methodologies to use for a roadmap engagement. The approach recommended in this chapter (and carrying on from Chapters 2 and 3 earlier in this book) is, in many ways, "methodology-neutral." That is, the major phases and activities presented below can be adjusted to fit specific phases of other methodologies.

Still, this book's approach is highly streamlined and based on the outcomes of more than 40 EDM-type roadmap efforts the author has been involved with over a period covering nearly 30 years. Our approach begins with the "pre-work" consisting of the rapid current state assessment (Chapter 2) and cataloguing EDM-relevant business initiatives (Chapter 3), and the proceeds to:

1. Address urgent current state issues
2. Define the first version of the EDM future state
3. Conduct a stakeholder summit for mid-engagement feedback
4. Adjust the EDM future state as necessary

5. Build the phased roadmap from the current state to the future state
6. Execute the roadmap

Figure 5.1 illustrates the six phases listed above, and the sections that follow describe each in more detail.

5.4 ADDRESS URGENT CURRENT STATE ISSUES

The current state assessment activities described in Chapter 2 are intended to quickly gather input from a broad collection of individuals for 16 key evaluation criteria: 4 categories (operational reporting and querying; strategic insights; data architecture; and work processes/human factors) and, for each of those 4 categories, 4 indexes:

- A complexity index
- A quality index
- A support index
- A tension index

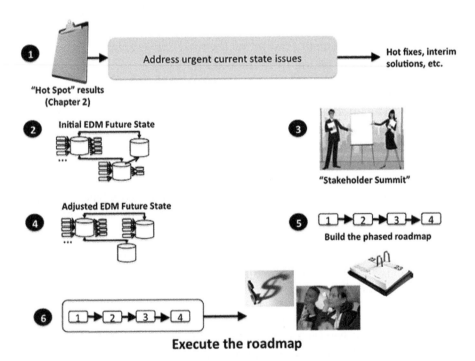

Fig. 5.1. The major activities of an EDM roadmap engagement.

As discussed in Chapter 2, one of the outcomes from the inputs and scoring was to identify any "hot spots" – i.e., precise areas that are particularly problematic in the current state, as indicated by an average index score of less than 2.5 (on a scale from 1:worst to 5:best).

While one of the key objectives of building an EDM roadmap is to address shortcomings in the enterprise's current state, some "hot spots" may actually be "too hot" – i.e., overwhelmingly problematic – to the point where corrective actions need to be taken *now*, not at some point identified on the future state roadmap. Perhaps the corrective actions will only be an interim solution: "bug fix" type patches that are out of step with the future EDM architecture, and will eventually need to be replaced by longer-term EDM capabilities that are aligned with the directions and future state architecture specified by the roadmap. Still, waiting to address one or more of the "hot spots" may be detrimental to the overall business.

As indicated in Figure 5.1, the first step in the EDM roadmap effort is to decide which, if any, "hot spots" need to be addressed now rather than waiting for the outcome of the roadmap effort...and then to proceed to do exactly that.

Even if an interim fix looks more like the proverbial "baling wire and chewing gum" solution – i.e., one that cannot be sustained for very long – at least the most significant EDM shortcomings in the current state can be addressed in a "stem the bleeding" manner. The interim solutions can then be factored into the roadmap effort where they will be replaced by ruggedized, architecturally compliant, "better" alternatives.

5.5 DEFINE THE INITIAL VERSION OF THE EDM FUTURE STATE

An all-too-common mistake, one likely made countless times over the years in hundreds or even thousands of EDM roadmap engagements, is to define the future state of enterprise data largely on the latest hot trends and concepts...whether proven or not, and also whether they are even relevant to a given organization (or not).

Figure 5.2 illustrates the key inputs the EDM roadmap team needs to consider when defining the future state...the second step of the EDM roadmap.

Each of the inputs shown in Figure 5.2 is described below.

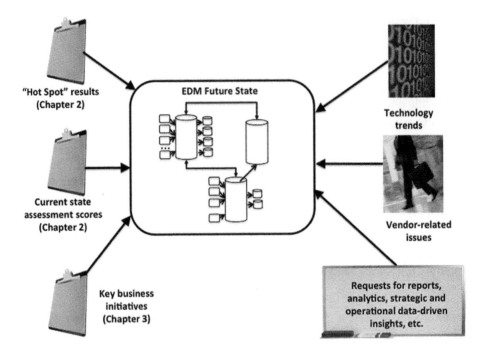

Fig. 5.2. Inputs used to define the initial EDM future state.

5.5.1 "Hot Spot" Results

As described earlier in this chapter, some EDM "hot spots" identified in the current state assessment may be so critical that interim repair-type solutions must be put in place *now* rather than wait until the future EDM architecture is defined and the roadmap finalized. Other "hot spots" may be problematic but, after careful consideration, can wait for architecturally compliant, roadmap-driven successors rather than urgent interim solutions that will almost certainly be decommissioned, despite the near-term work that goes into them.

All of the identified "hot spots" in the current state – whether tagged for near-term fixes or not – will be at the forefront of the key decisions made about the future EDM architecture. Referring back to Figure 2.8 in Chapter 2, an EDM team presented with the results from that particular current state assessment would have a full plate of items to focus on, and they can continually use the identified "hot spots" to ask themselves "are we addressing our most serious problems as we define our future state?"

5.5.2 Current State Assessment Scores

Even beyond the "hot spots," the current state scores from all 16 indexes present a very good set of guidelines for the EDM engagement team. Referring back to Figure 2.8 in Chapter 2, we see four indexes with scores around 3 (on the scale of 1:worst to 5:best) indicating that while there might be "adequate" quality for both operational reporting and strategic insights (e.g., business intelligence reports), and while support for both might also be acceptable, there is still plenty of room for improvement. As with those indexes that indicate "hot spots," each and every one of the indexes can provide constant guidance to help make sure that the EDM roadmap team is focused on improving not only what isn't working, but also what is only working to some extent.

Likewise, any current state index scores that are relatively high will provide guidance about capabilities and performance that need to be retained. Even if a given aspect of the current state will be replaced in the future state – an aging business intelligence tool with a new one, for example, or hand-written data interchange code with ETL and data replication tools – the team knows that new components and solutions need to meet the standards of performance and expectations of users and stakeholders. Essentially, backtracking and losing ground is highly undesirable, and the EDM roadmap team can focus on making sure that they at least meet, if not exceed, the capabilities in the current state that actually are working well.

5.5.3 Key Business Initiatives

Chapter 3 discussed how many key business initiatives need to have a strong underpinning of EDM to be successful. This checklist of those relevant to a given organization needs to be likewise factored into the definition of the future state. If strategic sourcing and other supply chain optimization (SCO) efforts are forthcoming, for example, the cohesiveness of supply chain-oriented data within the environment must be at the forefront of key architectural and design decisions. Likewise, the ability to deliver SCO-related reports and analytics as effortlessly as possible to key personnel involved in that value chain must be considered.

Or if an effort is underway to rationalize and consolidate multiple ERP and CRM applications into a single integrated portfolio, the future state needs to reflect the convergence and synthesis of the relevant current data stores into a cohesive enterprise systems data store. Additionally, the future state must reflect all of the necessary master data management (MDM), data governance, and other supporting capabilities necessary for the future integrated data state to operate effectively and not begin to degrade almost immediately after go-live.

5.5.4 Technology Trends

If this book were being written in the late 1980s and discussing how to build an EDM roadmap in that timeframe, you would likely find recommendations for:

- Beginning to migrate data from file systems and older, pointer-based database management systems to relational databases…initially for noncritical, support-type applications, and eventually mission-critical ones
- Possibly looking at distributed database management systems (DDBMS) technology to provide unified access to data stored in many different underlying database silos.

Or if we jump ahead to the mid-1990s, your future state for EDM would likely include:

- An all-encompassing, monolithic enterprise data warehouse – something like the picture shown in Figure 1.5 in Chapter 1 – to provide the bulk of strategic reporting and business intelligence for the enterprise
- But the lack of any sort of formalized MDM system

One more: let's go to the very late 1990s, in which we would likely find:

- One or more new ERP systems being implemented to resolve the Y2K problem, with plenty of custom-coded operational reports running directly off of the ERP databases
- New capabilities for eCommerce with siloed reporting and analysis driven by clickstream data, web logs, and other Internet-oriented data.

The point is that how an optimal future state architecture is defined is heavily influenced by the core technologies, architectural paradigms, leading products, and even conventional wisdom of that particular point in time. So as we look at the present day – the mid-2010s – we can certainly identify various components and architectural patterns that are *likely* to be present in a representative future state architecture, but EDM architects need to:

- Be wary of "bleeding edge" technologies that may not prove out (e.g., DDBMSs in the late 1980s/early 1990s)
- Make sure that so-called standardized architectures are actually relevant to their enterprise.

With regards to the latter, consider today's Big Data phenomenon. An emerging school of thought at the time of this book being written is that organizations should build what some call *data lakes*; i.e., Big Data-based stores of *all* of the enterprise's data. The premise behind a data lake is that with today's Big Data technology, the long-standing approach of feeding *certain* data into the reporting and analytical realm based on specific reporting and analytical requirements is obsolete. Some proponents of the data lake approach offer the premise that data lakes eliminate the need for data warehousing all together, and that simply "pouring all of the enterprise's data" into the data lake is all that needs to be considered for today's and tomorrow's enterprise data architecture.

Other analysts take a different approach: that Big Data-driven data lakes are valuable and "for real" but should coexist alongside data warehouses and data marts. Further, data lakes should be used to make predictive analytics and other forms of data mining part of any enterprise's mainstream usage and analysis of data, while data warehouses and the source systems themselves should still retain critical roles for operational reporting and traditional "tell me what happened and why" business intelligence.

For example, Bill Schmarzo, the Chief Technology Officer of EMC's Enterprise Information Management Service Line, proposes a composite architecture consisting of a Hadoop-based data store alongside a traditional ETL and also an "analytics sandbox" for exploratory data analysis (Schmarzo, 2013). Analyst Wayne Eckerson, the former Director of Research for TDWI (The Data Warehousing Institute) and a widely followed analyst, proposes a similar hybrid data lake-data warehouse architectural pattern in Eckerson, 2014), noting that while the tremendous interest in Big Data – Hadoop in particular – is certainly valid, enterprise data strategists and architects need to avoid jumping on the "no more data warehousing" bandwagon.

For purposes of defining a modern, mid-2010s EDM architecture to which an EDM roadmap will vector, strategists and architects need to consider *all* of the capabilities covered in Chapter 4, from traditional data warehousing to Big Data to MDM…and everything else mentioned in that chapter.

Not all capabilities will apply to every single enterprise, which brings us to another key point: aligning the future state architecture with the organization's structure and culture; its size; and other enterprise-specific factors.

5.5.5 Vendor-Related Issues

Sometimes vendor-related issues become significant factors in the future state architecture. For example, a given product vendor's software maintenance costs may have skyrocketed after that company was acquired by a much larger firm, and the vendor shows no interest at all in negotiating more favorable terms, even for long-standing customers.

Or perhaps a given enterprise has made a significant investment in the business intelligence and analysis tools of a given vendor that is later acquired by a larger firm, and the acquiring company eventually produces a roadmap that shows those tools on a path toward being "sunsetted" (i.e., on a trajectory toward no longer being supported).

For either of the above reasons, or a number of others, the future state architecture of an EDM roadmap effort may be influenced by vendor-related matters.

5.5.6 Requests Related to Reports and Analytics

An EDM roadmap is not the best vehicle to collect, validate, and prioritize detailed reporting and analytics requirements. Still, it's inevitable that the EDM roadmap team will hear feedback during individual interviews and group requirements sessions such as:

- "We need significantly more predictive analytics; almost all of the analysis we do is backwards-looking"

- "We need more self-service business intelligence in the hands of end users to cut down on our report development backlog"
- "We need to convert many of our tabular reports to dashboards and visualization"
- "We have no mobile BI capabilities right now, and we definitely need to start deploying BI on smart phones and tablets."

The EDM roadmap team will be able to use statements such as those above to help architect the future state for reporting, BI, and analytics (or, using the broader terminology of Chapter 4, *data retrieval, preparation, and delivery*).

5.6 CONDUCT THE STAKEHOLDERS' SUMMIT

At approximately the midpoint of the EDM roadmap engagement, a *Stakeholders' Summit* needs to occur. As one might expect from the title, a number of stakeholders, all of whom have some vested interest in the EDM roadmap effort and what comes next with regards to EDM, gather together for at least a half day to:

- Review the work accomplished to date
- Weigh in on the most significant open issues and decisions points
- Bring any underlying interorganizational or interpersonal tensions that may have been impacting the engagement work thus far to the surface
- Achieve consensus (or as high a degree of consensus as possible) as to the findings of the engagement team; preliminary recommendations; and the overall importance of seeing the engagement through to the end and then promptly beginning to execute the EDM roadmap.

Essentially, the Stakeholders' Summit establishes a "beachhead" from which the engagement team then moves forward – i.e., "breaks out from the beachhead" in military invasion terminology – for the remainder of the engagement without worrying that they will have to retrench and revisit topics for any one of a number of reasons: interorganizational politics; late-in-engagement surfacing of executive dissatisfaction with the quality of their work; or some other reason that throws the engagement into chaos.

5.7 ADJUST THE EDM FUTURE STATE AS NECESSARY

Using the feedback from the Stakeholders' Summit as well as outstanding to-do or to-research items, the EDM roadmap team can then adjust the future state architecture as necessary. If the team has done a thorough job in building the initial version of the future state, then only minor adjustments will typically need to be made before proceeding with the building of the phased roadmap (next phase).

5.8 BUILD THE PHASED ROADMAP

In any setting, for any sized company, the EDM roadmap should be an iterative, incremental, multiphase effort. Perhaps for a smaller-scale enterprise only two or three phases will be needed, with each phase of relatively short duration...with the entire effort accomplished in less than 1 year. Or for a much larger enterprise with a number of mission-critical, EDM-sensitive business initiatives in progress (Chapter 3), four or five phases over a 3- or 4-year period may be what is called for.

Every phase of the roadmap should contain:

- The body of work to be accomplished, along with minimum and maximum expected timeframes
- The complete list of all prerequisites that must be in place before that phase can commence, including all critical success factors (CSFs)
- A detailed analysis of all corequisites and touch-points with business initiatives, other technology initiatives...*anything* that could impact the success or failure of that phase's body of work
- The complete list of all products, platforms, technologies, etc. that will be used, along with necessary training for each
- Contingency plans if, for example, a data management product or analytics tool turns out not to "work as advertised"
- A complete list of all identified risks along with mitigation plans
- The necessary personnel resources along with specific roles and responsibilities of each individual
- Thoroughly defined criteria by which to declare that the phase was successful
- Program and project management models, policies, escalation paths, etc.

5.9 EXECUTE THE ROADMAP

Following completion of the EDM roadmap and acceptance by – ideally – the highest executive levels of the organization, the roadmap is then ready for execution. Ideally, as little time as possible should pass between the completion and acceptance of the EDM roadmap and beginning the body of work specified for its first phase.

Throughout the effort, the EDM strategists and architects need to be cognizant of the possibility of needing to make necessary adjustments. If, for example, one or more of the business imperatives discussed in Chapter 3 were to change, the EDM roadmap needs to be examined to determine if changes in priorities or phasing – or even the body of work – needs to occur as well. But all the while, the EDM leaders need to keep the effort moving forward, always with an eye toward regular and measurable progress toward the defined future state of EDM within the organization.

REFERENCES

Eckerson, W., 2014, Big Data Part III: Hadoop Will Not Kill the Data Warehouse – Beye NETWORK, April 10, http://www.b-eye-network.com/blogs/eckerson/.

Schmarzo, B., 2013, Modernizing Your Data Warehouse Part 2 – EMC² InFocus Blog, November 5, https://infocus.emc.com/william_schmarzo/modernizing-your-data-warehouse-part-2/.

CHAPTER 6

The End Game

6.1 INTRODUCTION

Delivering the future state identified in the enterprise data management (EDM) roadmap is a tremendous accomplishment for any organization. However, EDM-related work is far from over. This final chapter explores the "end game" of EDM: what comes next and how to sustain the hard-won gains.

6.2 ACHIEVING LASTING BUY-IN

Almost everyone who has played a key role in an enterprise-scale initiative has experienced situations where "not everyone is on the same page." The roadmap-stage consensus discussed in Chapter 5, supported by CxO mandates, will go a long way toward forging alliances across the enterprise that otherwise might not exist because of conflicting priorities, personalities, and similar reasons.

But what about going forward? Executives, directors, and managers come and go, as do architects and technology professionals. People get promoted into new roles, with new levels of authority. Reorganizations occur. Or an individual's perspective on the value of enterprise-scale data management may change over time, for any one of a variety of reasons.

Those chartered with managing and stewarding the EDM environment, or portions thereof, after the roadmap has been completed need to be well aware of the entire spectrum of individuals, roles, and perspectives that will support – or conversely, hinder – the EDM. The idea of a "friends and foes" list might sound Machiavellian (or like something out of the Nixon-era White House) but those in charge must have at least have some idea of who is an avid supporter of the EDM and who might, for whatever reason, be intent on disassembling part or all of what has been built.

No enterprise-scale initiative is ever "bullet-proof" against a deliberate, concerted effort to undermine what has been accomplished or even dismantle what has been built. But those in charge of the EDM can help guard against backtracking by:

- Regularly securing CxO "re-sponsorship" of the environment, with the CEO, COO, CIO, CFO, and others continuing to extol the business value delivered by the EDM environment.
- Maintaining an internal "sales deck" that concisely presents the business case for the EDM (that again, is already deployed and in use) to newly hired executives who may not have previously experienced the economies of scale and business value delivered by a well-functioning EDM environment, and may instead be more focused on their respective "fiefdoms" with regards to data, reports, analytics, etc.
- Vigilantly sustaining the overall quality, performance, and other characteristics of the EDM environment (see later in the chapter) to help prevent situations where one or more individuals can convincingly argue that the EDM environment cannot be trusted to meet their business needs, and thus they need to build and control their own data, reports, analytics, etc.

6.3 ARCHITECTURAL TUNE-UPS

Even a precisely architected and engineered EDM will, over time, find nonstandard products, interim solutions, patches, workarounds, and so on making their way into the environment for one reason or another. Perhaps a given capability needed to be added very quickly to meet a critical business need, and consequently "one-off" interfaces needed to be built rather than tapping into architected data flows.

Whatever the reasons, EDM owners need to guard against those interim solutions, workarounds, etc. becoming entrenched and expanding over time to the point where the architectural integrity of the EDM is compromised. One approach to addressing this situation is to periodically conduct an *architectural tune-up* effort.

For a period of approximately 3 months, new development and capabilities housed in and managed by the EDM are frozen...at least as much as possible given the state of the overall business. Or, at the very least, new development is cordoned off into a tightly bound segment of the EDM where those activities can be compartmentalized while the rest of the EDM is "tuned up."

Workarounds will be remediated to architecturally compliant components and data flows; interim solutions that may lack full architectural rigor will be enhanced to be compliant with EDM standards; databases that have seen degradation of their performance will have their physical schemas restructured; ETL job-streams will be reorganized to address problems such as exceeding batch windows that may have become increasingly frequent, delaying the delivery of critical morning operational reports; and so on.

Ideally, architectural tune-ups should be accomplished every 18–24 months. (Of course, ongoing database tuning, performance monitoring, etc. will be occurring all along the way to address the most immediate problems.)

A paradigm for the architectural tune-up is the United States Air Force's B-52 bomber. Originally designed in the mid-1940s and deployed in the 1950s, the B-52 of today has been rearchitected and redesigned over and over *on the same airframe* to the point where the planes are expected to serve into the 2040s! On the outside, the B-52 of today (and tomorrow) looks very similar to that of the Eisenhower era even though its technology has dramatically evolved to support many new missions never originally envisioned.

An EDM environment that was built according to a well-architected roadmap *and which is properly maintained, including regular "tune-ups"* can likewise stay in existence for many years and be regularly enhanced to support new "data missions."

6.4 DEALING WITH DISRUPTIVE SEISMIC EVENTS

Technology professionals who have been in the working world for more than a couple of years have already experienced the impact of at least one seismic events: specifically, the Great Recession that began in 2007–2008 and which, for a couple of years, played havoc with IT budgets and initiatives. Those who have been in the working world for longer periods of time may also have experienced:

- The emergence of the Internet and web technology
- The race to resolve Y2K compliance in software and data
- The dot-com meltdown in 2000
- The economic aftermath of the 9/11 terrorist attacks
- The aftermath of various accounting scandals in the early 2000s

Indeed, one can go back further in history and find other seismic events such as the Great Depression, World War II, the post-war boom years, the oil shocks and recessions of the 1970s, the PC revolution of the 1980s...all of which dramatically impacted business, technology, and conventional wisdom.[1]

The point is that no matter how foresightful strategists might be, or how flexibly-architected any environment – EDM or otherwise – might be to handle murky future possibilities, highly disruptive seismic events seem to regularly occur. Some of these seismic events are positive in nature: the economic booms of the 1980s and 1990s for example, with plentiful budgets available to capitalize on technological advances and further enhance a company's fortunes in flush economic times. Other seismic events are ominous, with the inevitable consequence of budget cuts and stalled or canceled initiatives in the face of difficult times.

EDM owners need to be fully aware of both positive and negative seismic events that are disruptive to whatever plans are in place for their respective environments. Positive disruption can be seized upon, with the EDM's trajectory adjusted as necessary to take advantage of what may have burst on the scene. The Big Data era is a very good example. Organizations with well-architected data warehousing and overall data management capabilities are typically more likely to be able to experiment with Hadoop and other Big Data technologies and incorporate those capabilities into their overall environments in an orderly manner, without having to go back to the drawing board.

---

[1] One can go even further back in American history and consider the Industrial Revolution, or the various "panics" – the then-used term for economic depressions or severe recessions – as seismic events.

Conversely, enterprises hallmarked by a patchwork of nonintegrated data marts, spreadmarts proliferation, and other less-than-desirable EDM characteristics often have no way for Big Data to converge with their current state. (Thus, the purpose of this book…to build a roadmap building from whatever one's current EDM state might be, whether well-functioning or not.)

6.5 MANAGING VENDOR RELATIONSHIPS

As with most individuals with leadership roles in a technology-driven business initiative, EDM leaders will have plenty of opportunities to interact with people from the various product vendors they use, as well as numerous others who wish to secure some sort of role for their products in any given EDM environment. Most of the interactions will be with people in sales-focused roles: account managers, pre-sales product specialists, regional sales managers, etc.

EDM leaders need to broaden their relationships with their vendor partners to include individuals such as product managers, who "own" (or at least have a significant role in) a given product's roadmap, feature set, upcoming new interfaces, and overall future capabilities. EDM leaders should insist on building relationships with and having access to product managers (as well as overall product management executives whose responsibility may span multiple products) to discuss product direction; capabilities not working as promised; difficulties working with software development frameworks…pretty much anything that is critical to the success of *their* respective EDM initiatives.

The information technology world has seen many occasions where specific products or even entire computing companies have taken a significant misstep or misread the overall market direction (the often-cited classic example: Digital Equipment Corporation in the late 1980s and early 1990s with PCs and Unix) and adversely impacted not only their own fates but the health of their customers' computing environments. EDM owners and leaders need to proactively manage these vendor relationships to the point where they are confident their vendor partners are in lockstep with marketplace forces and overall technology shifts.

6.6 ETERNAL VIGILANCE

All of the topics covered above come together under a single, overarching theme: eternal vigilance. From (1) data quality throughout the EDM environment to (2) the usage of specific BI or data management products to (3) doing one's best to prevent organizational politics from undoing hard-won gains, one might paraphrase the famous saying "eternal vigilance is the price of liberty" as:

> *Eternal vigilance is the price required to help ensure that a well-architected, successful enterprise data management environment continues to succeed at its business and technology missions for years to come.*

Or, in search of an appropriate companion phrase to close this book – and taking a trip back in time nearly 250 years – we find Thomas Paine's "Those who expect to reap the blessings of freedom must, like men, undergo the fatigue of supporting it" (Paine, 1777) – which we might modernize and apply to the subject of EDM in this manner:

> *Those who expect to reap the benefits of the enterprise data management environment they have built must, like professionals, undergo the fatigue of supporting it.*

REFERENCE

Paine, T., The American Crisis, Number 4, September 12, 1777.

Further Resources and References

Many of the topics covered in this book are discussed in greater detail in various white papers, academic journal papers, and articles. Additionally, many blogs cover enterprise data management-related topics and are available for the reader to follow.

The list of resources and references below is by no means exhaustive but rather is meant to be representative. Enterprise data management is a rapidly evolving discipline, especially with the "Dawn of the Big Data Era" upon us.

WHITE PAPERS

Nearly every data management product vendor, consultancy, and industry specialty group produces white papers on a regular basis. Readers certainly need to keep in mind that white papers often present a particular point of view favorable to the specific product and service offerings available from whomever is writing or sponsoring the paper, but at the same time many white papers are content-rich and spark valuable insights into the reader's own enterprise data management environment.

Representative white papers that are particularly content-rich with regards to enterprise data management include:

- "Big Data and Enterprise Data: Bridging Two Worlds with Oracle Data Integration" – Oracle Corporation, September, 2013.
- "The Microsoft Modern Data Warehouse" – Microsoft Corporation, 2013.
- "Best Practices Report: Evolving Data Warehouse Architectures in the Age of Big Data" – TDWI Research, Second Quarter 2014.
- "Use Big Data Technologies to Modernize Your Enterprise Data Warehouse" – EMC Corporation, August, 2012.

PERIODICALS

- *Information Management* – available at http://www. information-management.com/
- IBM Data Magazine – available at http://ibmdatamag.com/ (IBM-centric)
- Computerworld – available at http://www.computerworld.com/ (general computing but also containing regular data management content)

BLOGS

Blogs authored by thought leaders in various aspects of enterprise data management often give good insight into trends, what's working and what isn't, and other up-to-the-minute information. Blogs of interest to the topic of EDM include:

- Beye Network blogs: www.b-eye-network.com/blogs include contributions from Wayne Eckerson, Barry Devlin, Steve Dine, Jill Dyche, and others
- Bill Schmarzo blog: infocus.emc.com/author/william_schmarzo

INDUSTRY GROUPS

- TDWI (The Data Warehousing Institute) – http://tdwi.org/ Home.aspx
- DAMA (Data Management Association) – www.dama.org

Printed and bound by CPI Group (UK) Ltd, Croydon, CR0 4YY

03/10/2024

01040423-0006